The ZOO in the garden

Discover the animals which live in your garden

David Taylor & Mike Birkhead

Introduction

You may not know it, but you share your garden with lots of other living creatures – you can observe *THE ZOO IN THE GARDEN* from your doorstep.

Many of the animals in the garden seem common or everyday, but in fact they are part of an intricate web of life, each an expert surviving in its own style. So read on and find out about what lives in YOUR garden.

First published in Great Britain in 1987
by Boxtree Limited

Text copyright © 1987 by David Taylor
Photographs copyright © 1987 by Mike Birkhead

ISBN 1 85283 002 6

Edited by Graham Eyre
Designed by Grahame Dudley
Typeset by Servis Filmsetting Limited, Manchester

Printed in Italy by New Interlitho S.p.A. - Milan

for Boxtree Limited, 25, Floral Street,
London WC2E 9DS

Acknowledgement
Photo on page 30 courtesy Oxford Scientific Films

Contents

The Blue Tit	6
The Hedgehog	8
The Mole	12
The Blackbird	16
The Ladybird	20
The Centipede and Millipede	24
The Butterfly	28
The Bee	34
The Frog	38
The Snail	42

Abbreviations

mm millimetre
cm centimetre
m metre
km kilometre
ha hectare
gm gram
kg kilogram

The Blue Tit

One of the handsomest of Britain's garden birds is this little dandy in its blue, yellow, black and white gear. If blue tits were a rare tropical species, folk would no doubt praise their beauty more loudly. As it is, the blue tit is the fourth most common bird to be seen in gardens in Britain. Only the blackbird, starling and house sparrow are more common.

The name 'blue tit' is a shortened form of 'blue titmouse' and 'titmouse' comes from Old English. 'Tit' means tiny and 'mouse' (nothing to do with Mickey Mouse!) is a corruption of 'mose', meaning a small bird. Tits, of which there are 42 species worldwide, are typical insect-eating birds of scrub and woodland. Our friend the blue tit occurs widely throughout Europe and Asia.

The blue tit is ever active, tending to flit about from branch to branch, but able to fly long distances too. It is an expert at hanging upside-down, which enables it to hunt caterpillars on the underside of leaves. You can watch its acrobatics for yourself if you have a hanging container of bird food (nuts, suet or one of the special mixtures available from the pet or garden shop) in your garden or back-yard – especially in the winter months, when there are not many insects about and blue tits rely more on seeds and berries for food. At the end of summer, blue tits tend to leave the garden and go hunting in groups in woodland, but they are back as soon as the winter cold sets in.

A pair of blue-tit parents feeding their nestlings gather caterpillars at a rate of around 1 per minute. That means that over the whole period of raising their chicks they catch about 10,000 caterpillars! Another thing blue tits like is cream. They are often seen making short work of milk-bottle tops and helping themselves to the cream at the top of the bottle.

Blue-tit eggs are laid in clutches averaging 10 in number, but they can range from as few as 6 to as many as 24. The eggs, which are white with reddish-brown spots, are laid in April or May and hatch at a time when there are lots of caterpillars around for the chicks to eat. The incubation period – the time it takes for the eggs to hatch – is around 12–14 days and only the female sits on the eggs to hatch them.

About 1 month after the eggs hatch you may be lucky enough to watch the young birds trying to pluck up courage to leave the nest for the first time. To tempt her youngsters to fly, the mother bird sits on a convenient perch outside the nest with a plump caterpillar in her beak. She gives lots of encouragement to her children, saying in effect, 'Come on! You can do it, and here's the prize for the first one to prove it!' The first fledgling to leave the nest is the one who hesitates the most, but as soon as it

A blue tit, the fourth commonest bird in our garden, takes wing

Blue tits welcome feeding in winter

takes the plunge the others usually all fly out at once.

Like other tits, the blue tit nests in a hole in a tree-trunk or, if you are lucky, in your garden nest-box. The nest, which must be dry and draught-proof is snugly lined with shreds of wool, feathers, hair, dried grass and moss. Nest-boxes should have a hole, metal-rimmed to prevent squirrels or woodpeckers from making it bigger, no more than 2.8 cm across (to keep out starlings and sparrows). Excellent ones can be obtained from the Royal Society for the Protection of Birds. The box should be placed in a position facing away from the prevailing winds at a height of between 1.5 and 2 m with plenty of space around – blue tits like to keep an eye open for their enemies.

Mother as flying-instructor!

Nest-boxes need sound construction

The Hedgehog

The hedgehog is not found in America but is widespread across Europe (except for most of Scandinavia and Iceland), Africa and Asia. There are 12 different species of hedgehog, including the *Western European* (the welcome visitor to our garden), the *long-eared hedgehog* and the *desert hedgehog*. The hedgehog is Britain's heaviest insectivore (insect-eating animal), weighing up to 1.4 kg, and measuring up to 30 cm in length. Hedgehog spines are actually very

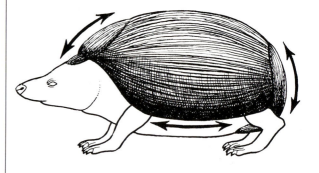

The muscle-shield of the hedgehog

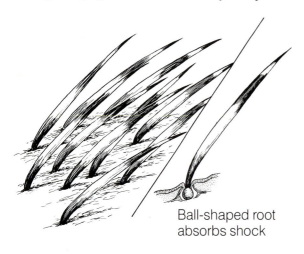

Ball-shaped root absorbs shock

The shock-absorbing spine of a hedgehog

Heading for trouble

strong and flexible hairs and each adult animal sports about 6000 of them. They are 2–3 cm long, and each has a ball-like root to take shocks and a muscle that can pull it upright when the hedgehog is alarmed. Hedgehogs curl up into a ball at any sign of danger; that's why so many are tragically squashed on our roads. To curl up, a hedgehog uses a big oval shield of muscles that lies beneath the skin, over the back and down the sides of the body from head to tail. By

Our friend relishes some cat food

drawing in this shield, rather like pulling on the draw-string of a bag, the animal is instantly transformed into a spiky ball.

Hedgehogs are a gardener's friend, feeding on grubs, snails, caterpillars and other pests. Their favourite dish is worms, but they will also eat insects, woodlice, spiders, snails, frogs, toads, lizards and snakes, as well as berries, seeds or fallen fruit, though they do *not*, despite the charming legend, roll about in orchards spearing apples and pears on their prickles and then carrying them off to their larders. If you wish to put out food for a visiting hedgehog, try a saucer of milk, a bit of tinned cat or dog food, hard-boiled egg or cheese scraps. Hedgehogs do take wild birds' eggs if they come across them, but I don't believe they enter hen pens and steal or devour unbroken hens' eggs. As for the belief that hedgehogs suckle milk from cows, I think that's nonsense too. But sometimes a hedgehog may come across a cow with a little milk oozing from the teat of a full udder and lap up the drops.

Hedgehogs are very resistant to many kinds of poison. They can survive the bites of snakes that would kill 10 men and can eat wasps and bees without apparently being troubled by the insects' stings. They are also very noisy: they snort, hiss, cough cackle, puff, grunt and scream. Nobody who has never heard a hedgehog would believe how noisy it can be. Hedgehogs have fairly good eyesight, but scientists report that they see the world only in shades of yellow! Their senses of hearing and smell are wonderfully well developed. When a hedgehog starts sniffing about, its nose begins to run and this helps the lining of its nostrils to pick up more efficiently the scents in the air.

Hedgehogs are fine swimmers but don't usually take a dip unless they have to. They are also surprisingly good climbers, and when they want to descend they simply let themselves roll

Hedgehogs are quite good climbers

down, using their spines as shock-absorbers. Few enemies can penetrate the spiky defensive ball of a curled-up hedgehog. Foxes and dogs stand little chance. Badgers, polecats or martens and large birds of prey (such as eagles) may sometimes be successful in forcing the ball open.

Hedgehogs hibernate in the winter, usually going to sleep in October and waking up in April. They pick a snug place called a 'hibernaculum' in a pile of dried leaves or a hole in a bank that they line with moss, bracken and leaves. To save energy and make sure the food stored in its body lasts till spring, the animal allows its temperature to drop and its heartbeat and breathing-rate slow right down. Beneath the skin of the hedgehog's back there is a special hibernation food source in the form of a layer of brown fat. This fat can release heat 20 times faster than ordinary fat and acts as if controlled by a thermostat. The lower the outside temperature, the more heat the brown fat releases into the sleeping hedgehog's body.

In spring a mother hedgehog makes

Napping away the winter months

A prickly defensive ball

her nest in some quiet spot, which may, if you are lucky, be beneath the floor of a garden shed. The baby hedgehogs are born between May and July, with a second litter sometimes produced during August and September after a pregnancy period of 30–40 days. There are normally 3–7 blind and deaf babies in a litter, each of them weighing about 9 gm. The spines of a newborn baby hedgehog are pale, soft and rubbery and are flattened into the skin, which is especially soggy with a high water content. $1\frac{1}{2}$–3 days after birth a second layer of spines begins to grow through the first spines, which are now standing upright. A baby hedgehog cannot roll into a ball until it is about 10 days old.

If you handle a hedgehog – perhaps nursing an injured one – be careful of any fleas and other parasites that there may be on the skin between the spines.

The Mole

The mole is that curious little fellow whose activities make lumps on the lawn. Because it works underground in the dark, and so is rarely seen, the mole is the least known of British garden mammals, though to my mind that makes it one of the most intriguing. It used to be trapped a lot for its velvety fur, used to make coats and trousers, but happily that has nearly stopped.

There are a number of different species of mole. The only one who lives in Britain is the *European mole*. In Spain, the Balkans and Turkey is found the *Mediterranean* mole, and the *Roman mole* lives in Italy and the Balkans. One of the most curious species is the *star-nosed mole* of North America, who looks as if he has a flower growing on the end of his snout.

A mole's body is long and perfectly shaped for the job of tunnelling. Its colour is a uniform black or dark grey with a short fur whose hairs are of even length and can lie flat in any direction (again, useful for tunnelling). The long, pointed muzzle is hairless except for the specialized, highly sensitive whiskers and can be wiggled about.

Moles have tiny but completely formed eyes. They cannot see very well, but their eyes are sensitive to changes in the brightness of light. Moles, which have no external ears, have a poorly developed sense of hearing, as you would expect of a creature who lives mostly underground, but they need and have a very good sense of smell. Glands in the animal's groin produce a smelly substance which is smeared by the belly fur onto the floor of the mole's underground tunnels, as a chemical sign that they are private property. The smell fades quite quickly and must be renewed regularly to keep up the effect. The most powerful sense of the mole, however, is that of touch. Life underground depends on a highly developed ability to feel your way round and recognize obstacles. The mole's

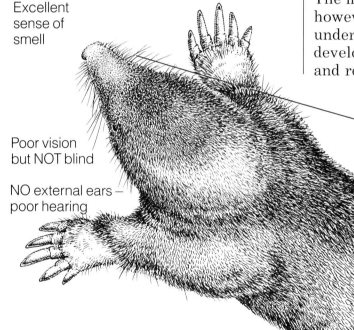

A mole's senses

- Excellent sense of smell
- Poor vision but NOT blind
- NO external ears – poor hearing
- Highly touch-sensitive whiskers

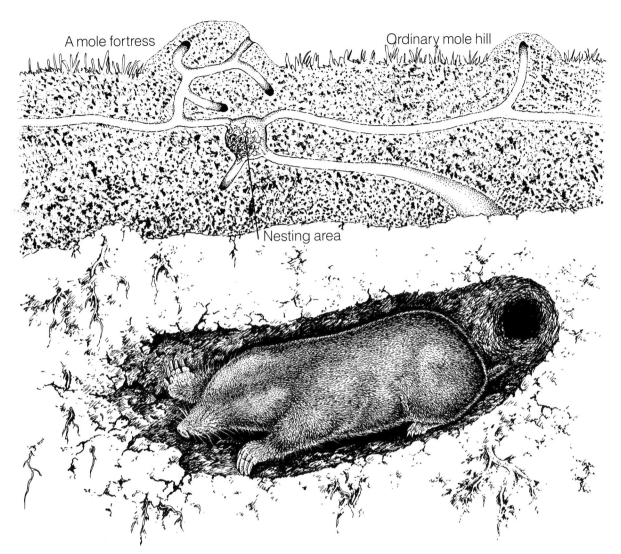

A mole is an expert miner. He constructs his own underground system

muzzle has nerve-endings and there are prominent, very sensitive whiskers on the muzzle and tail.

The powerful digging ability of the mole lies in its sturdy fore-limbs, which are always turned outwards and have five strong, long claws. Moles dig permanent tunnels beneath the soil, with a central nest area lined with grass and leaves. There are occasional shafts up to the surface. Molehills are the earth thrown up on the surface from these shafts. Sometimes in damp soils a special sort of molehill, the fortress, is built to contain the central nesting-area. Tunnels may be up to 1 m deep, and usually the area in which one mole makes its tunnels do not overlap much with the territories of other moles. Moles live alone except in the mating season, though they do seem to be aware of the presence of other moles nearby. Occasionally if there is a drought they are forced to leave their tunnel system and travel perhaps as far as 1 km to find water, a journey which may take them across the territories of up to 10 other moles. When one mole dies or is removed from its patch, its scent fades rapidly and the chemical warning telling other moles to keep away disappears. Other moles quickly take over the property. Sometimes one neighbour takes over the whole territory. Sometimes it is split up among several moles. There may be 5–25 moles per hectare of land, depending upon the soil quality, drainage and the availablity of food. Moles outside the mating season are very unfriendly and fight furiously if they come across other moles.

A mole feeds on worms, slugs, beetles and insect larvae, most of which it finds as it patrols its tunnel system. If not enough food is available, the mole may dig some new tunnels. One adult animal can eat up to 50 gm of worms per day and it will store living worms (paralysed but not killed by having their heads bitten off) in a larder chamber near to the nest. This is done particularly in late autumn as a source of food during the winter.

Moles are active day and night. In

A rare sight! A mole above ground

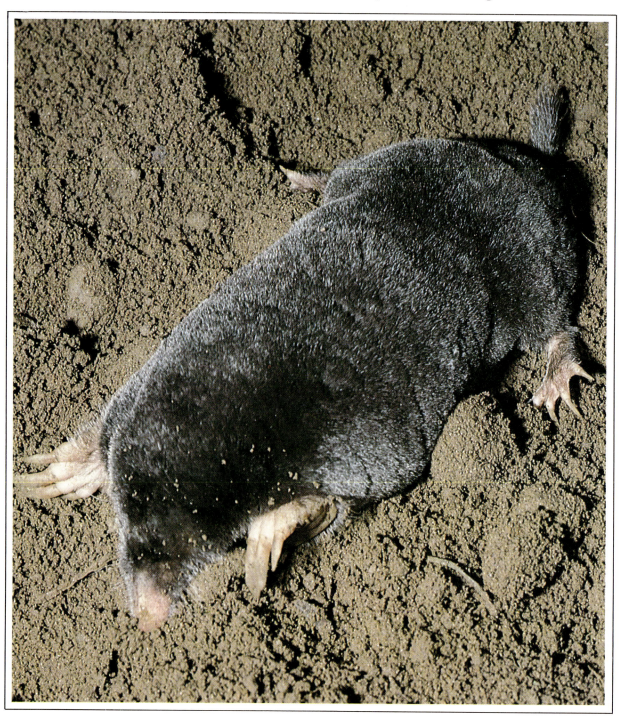

A mole's skin is soft as velvet

winter both males and females work in the tunnels and sleep in their nests in 4-hour spells, which begin when they leave the nest around sunrise. Females do this all year round except in summer, when they are suckling their young and need to go back to the nest more often. During spring, males tend to sleep for short periods in their tunnels and spend much of the rest of their time looking for a mate. At this time they may not visit their nests for days on end. In summer they go back to the pattern of 4 hours' work, 4 hours' sleep, and then in autumn they become lazier and are active for only 2 periods of 4 hours a day. You might wonder how scientists have learnt all this about the mole's underground daily routine. The answer is that they have attached harmless radio transmitters to captured moles; the transmitters tell the scientists what the moles are doing once they have been set free again.

British moles mate between March and June. Surprisingly, since the mole lives underground, the breeding activity is controlled by the amount of daylight! We assume that the mole detects this when it comes to the surface, as it occasionally does when looking for nesting material, and that daylight acts as a signal to the mole's body that it is time to mate if a partner can be found. The young are born in litters of 2–7 after a pregnancy of 1 month. They are born naked but develop fur by the end of their second week of life. Their eyes open at the end of the third week and they suckle their mother's milk for a total of 4–6 weeks. Then they leave their mother's nest and wander off above ground in search of territory they can dig and claim for their own. It is at this time that large numbers (perhaps over half) of young moles are caught and killed by their enemies, including man. Moles are regarded as pests by gardeners and groundsmen, not only because of the damage molehills do to lawns and sports fields, but also because tunnelling by moles can harm the roots of young plants. Traps and poisons are used in attempts to kill moles.

A mole catcher

The Blackbird

Widespread and numerous in Great Britain, with even more migrating across the English Channel during the winter, this wonderful songbird (I vote it the best of native British songsters) is familiar to everyone. The male is easily recognizable – black with a yellow bill and a yellow ring around the eye. The female is perhaps less easily identified, being dark brown with a pale throat, dark bill and again a yellow ring around the eye. Young birds resemble the females but are generally paler and more mottled. Oddly enough, white blackbirds sometimes occur, though nearly all of these are only partly white, not true albinos (creatures lacking all colour).

Blackbirds are members of the thrush family, which includes 63 different species worldwide. They are intelligent birds that clearly regard the garden as their own and have little fear of human beings. They hop about the lawn and flowerbeds, stopping from time to time to cock their head and listen for the sound of worms moving underground. (They have very sharp hearing.) If they hear anything they will do a bit of digging, making shallow scrapes with their feet and pecking at the ground with their bill. They turn over leaves looking for insects and snails and search bushes and low trees for soft fruit. They tend to fly low, swerving

A male blackbird in typical pose

effortlessly round bushes and landing with tails held up and wings drooping.

Blackbirds are very territorial: they keep to what they consider their own plot of land, and chase other blackbirds off. So, if you have a pair of blackbirds in your garden, you will see a lot of them. If you have a garden pool or birdbath you will be able to see your blackbirds taking their daily bath and obviously enjoying it. A blackbird having a bath sits well down in the water, fluffing out its feathers, lifting and flapping its wings, flicking water over its back with its beak and then nibbling at its breast plumage. It's all done in quick fussy bursts, after which the bird flies off to its favourite spot for drying and preening – a branch or place on the fence close by. Shaking itself and fluffing up its feathers, the bird turns its head and prods with its beak at its preen gland, near the base of its tail. This gland contains waterproofing oil, which the prodding releases. The beak transfers the oil to the wing and body feathers, smearing them with a fine

Blackbirds love berries

The preen gland of a bird. It provides the oil for waterproofing

The preen gland here contains waterproofing oil

'Anting' – to keep down parasites

A female on her deep nest of grass and leaves

coating in a rapid series of nibbling movements.

In warm weather the blackbird will also do a bit of garden sunbathing, and, if there's a patch of sand or dust around, it will take the opportunity to have a dustbath, which keeps the feathers in good condition. You may also see a blackbird crouching with wings spread in a dry part of the garden allowing ants to run all over it. This apparently strange behaviour, called 'anting', is a form of pest control: the ants secrete an acid from glands at the rear of their abdomens and this kills off unwanted guests of the blackbird such as feather mites.

At breeding-time, blackbirds build a deep nest of grass and leaves, usually lightly cemented with mud and situated in a bush, climbing plant or garden shed. Nesting occurs earlier in gardens than in woodlands. The eggs, which are light blue-green with reddish speckles, are laid between March and July in 2 or 3 clutches of 3–6 eggs. The female incubates the eggs and the youngsters start to fly at about 2 weeks old.

The old nursery-rhyme 'Sing a Song of Sixpence' mentions 'four and twenty blackbirds baked in a pie'. Many old nursery rhymes are like secret messages that you cannot understand unless you know the code, and this is true of 'Sing a Song of Sixpence'. It may refer to King Henry VIII, who in the sixteenth century decided to close down all the monasteries in England. The blackbirds may be the monasteries' choirs; the Queen in the parlour eating bread and honey may be Catherine of Aragon, Henry's first wife; and the maid hanging out the clothes may be Henry's second wife, Ann Boleyn.

A children's rhyme with a hidden meaning

The Ladybird

Not many people like insects, but, then, most people think of insects as nasty creepy-crawlies. In fact there are some very beautiful insects, such as butterflies, dragonflies and scarab beetles (which come from the East and have shells so lovely that they have been used as jewellery). These are the sort of insects nearly everyone likes, though few realize that they are insects. The same is true of the beetle called the ladybird. The 'lady' in its name refers to the Virgin Mary ('Our Lady') and the 'bird' here just means a flying creature.

If a ladybird lands on you, then according to an old English tradition you are supposed not to flick it off but to blow gently and say,

Ladybird, ladybird, fly away home.
Your house is on fire and your
    children are gone.

It is thought that this verse refers to the old practice of setting fire to hop fields in September after the harvest.

In Northumberland in the north of England, where an old name for the ladybird is the 'reed sodger', there is a similar tradition. You throw the ladybird into the air and say,

Reed, reed sodger fly away
And make the morn a sunny day.

French children recite a verse that

A seven-spot out and about

warns the ladybird of a Turkish invasion and the slaughter of all her young ones. Everywhere the ladybird is regarded as a good and useful creature, feeding as it does on both the larvae and adult forms of aphids – pests such as the greenfly. The number of spots on a ladybird's wings was thought to indicate

The basic insect body and a ladybird compared. The ladybird uses one pair of wings as a wing-case

the future price of wheat: each spot represented an extra shilling for a bushel of corn (5 pence for 36 litres). It was considered particularly unlucky to kill a ladybird, and in East Anglia, for example, if one were accidentally killed it would be carefully buried and the grave stamped upon 3 times while the rhyme 'Ladybird, ladybird, fly away home' was recited. At one time the yellow liquid which the insect secretes when alarmed was considered an effective treatment for toothache. The sufferer rubbed his finger on the ladybird's legs and then rubbed the liquid onto the aching tooth.

Like other insects, ladybirds are creatures that live on land, have no backbones or lungs, and breathe through a system of simple air-tubes that open onto the body surface. The body is divided into three main parts – the head, the chest or thorax, and the abdomen. It is covered by a horny coating or external skeleton which is shed now and again to allow the insect to grow. The head carries a pair of feelers or antennae and there are three pairs of feeding appendages. Generally there are one or two pairs of wings arising from the thorax and three pairs of legs.

True beetles, of which there are around 300,000 species, form the biggest group of insects, and range in size from 0.5 mm to over 15 cm long. The largest are the *Goliath beetles*, which are some of the biggest insects alive. The Latin name (*Coleoptera*) of the beetle family means 'sheath wings' and refers to the fore-wings, which form an armoured covering for the delicate hind wings used for flying. Beetles live mainly on the ground and have a heavily armed head with a mouth formed for biting and compound eyes, which allow the beetle

The ladybird is a carnivore, not a plant-eater

to see almost all the way round itself.

There are 400 species of ladybird in the world and there are 41 species in Great Britain. All are round in outline with hemispherical bodies (like an up-turned pudding bowl) where the head is concealed beneath the thorax. Most are brightly coloured and spotted. They have short and nimble legs. Nearly all are carnivorous, which means that they eat other animals. Ladybirds are indeed gardeners' friends, though there are a few exceptions: for instance, the squash ladybird of the United States damages pumpkins. The striking colours and designs of ladybirds serve to warn creatures that might be tempted to eat them that they contain poisonous chemicals, though no human can be harmed by handling them.

If you look carefully you may be able to identify 5 or 6 different species of ladybird busily going about their business of keeping down the greenfly in your garden. One of the commonest is the *seven-spot ladybird*, which is about 6 mm long and has 3 black spots on each of its bright red wing-cases, with the seventh spot shared between them. You will often find this ladybird resting under a flower-head. A plant it is particularly fond of is hogweed. The biggest ladybird in Britain is the *eyed ladybird*, about 8 mm long. It is frequently found on pine-trees and displays 7 or 8 spots on each wing-case. The most common British ladybird is the *two-spot*. Generally it has one spot on each wing-case, but just to confuse you it may have a total of 4 or even 6! Some varieties reverse the colouring by having red spots on black wing-cases. The *ten-spot ladybird* is also quite common and tends to favour woodland. It possesses red, brown or black wing-cases with yellow, black or orange spots. It is about 4 mm long and has tiny yellow legs. In southern parts of England the *fourteen-spot ladybird* can sometimes be found. It is about 4 mm long and has very bright and distinct yellow and black markings. Smaller still at 3 mm long is the *twenty-two spot ladybird*, which has 11 black spots on each yellow or pale orange wing-case. It can be found in certain areas of England, Wales and eastern Ireland.

A twenty-two spot ladybird

A fourteen-spot ladybird with spots fused together

The *twenty-four spot ladybird* is an interesting creature, being a vegetarian that feeds on clover and similar plants. Despite its name, it has a total of 16–20 irregularly sized spots on its orange wing-cases. It is another of the smaller ladybirds, at around 3 mm long.

Although ladybirds tend to remain calm with their wing-cases closed when you pick one up or gently touch one sitting on a flower, they are very good at flying. Their finely veined transparent hind wings can carry them over vast distances. Some ladybirds migrate to Britain from continental Europe and occasionally a swarm of them can number tens of thousands. If they are unlucky enough to meet with bad weather on the way, so many of them may fall into the sea that the water seems to turn red.

Adult ladybirds hibernate over winter in Great Britain. Look for them beneath pieces of loose bark or on the underside of dry and sheltered window-sills. Many die of diseases such as fungus infections. They also have an enemy in the form of a wasp-like insect that lays its eggs within the body of the adult ladybird. When the eggs hatch into grubs they feed on the flesh of the ladybird but do not necessarily kill it. Sometimes you will see the tiny pupa of the parasite still attached to a ladybird as it works its way along a stem full of greenfly.

Each female ladybird lays about 200 eggs, generally on the underside of leaves and conveniently near to greenfly colonies. Larvae emerge from the eggs and begin feeding on the aphids, killing perhaps 30 or 40 every day. The larval ladybird, a slate-blue caterpillar-like creature with yellow spots, grows to be much longer than the adult beetle at around 12–13 mm. In the 3 weeks before the larva turns into a pupa it eats it way through many hundreds of aphids. At the end of the 3 weeks the larva shrinks and rounds off into a hard-cased grey and yellow oval pupa, rather like a button. The pupa is firmly attached to a stem of leaf, generally in an exposed position, and stays there until the adult ladybird emerges from it.

The baby is longer than the adult!

The Centipede and Millipede

Do a bit of digging and you will soon enough come across a flattish, rusty-brown, many-legged creature that wriggles artfully away from your trowel or spade. It is the centipede, and, like the ladybird, it is a friend of the gardener. Centipedes are not insects – though, funnily enough, they are more closely related to insects than to the somewhat similar millipedes. There are around 3000 species of centipede. Almost all of them live on the land and have elongated bodies made up of many segments, with a distinct head, one pair of feelers or antennae, and a single pair of legs on each segment. As most species are carnivorous, preying upon small animals such as slugs and insects, they help to control plant pests in the garden. Like insects, spiders and Crustaceans (such as lobsters and crabs) centipedes have their skeletons on the outside of the body in the form of a tough outer shell or 'exoskeleton'. This cannot stretch, so the centipede has to shed its body covering from time to time to be able to grow. The cast-off outer skeletons are whitish and hollow, and look rather 'ghostly'. You may be able to find them lying in the garden.

Although the word 'centipede' means 'a hundred feet', the number of feet varies from 34 and 254, depending on the species. The longest known species is a 46-legged giant living in the jungles of South America, which when fully grown is about 40 cm long but can reach 90 cm! Big centipedes such as this are fully grown at around 4 years old and may live for 10 years. British centipedes, of which there are 44 species, don't get

The centipede is blind as a bat

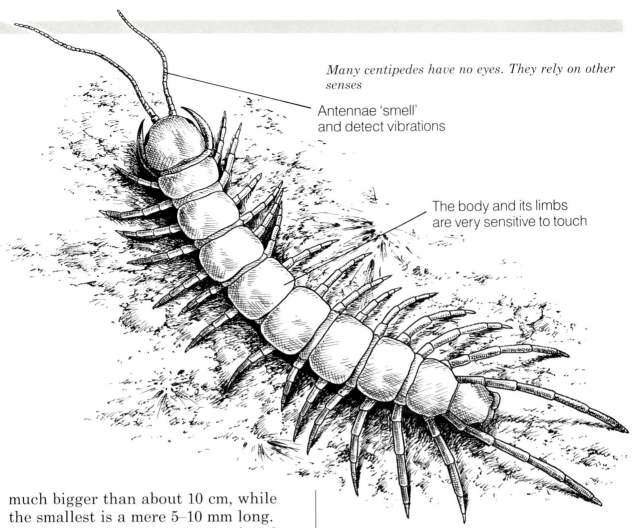

Many centipedes have no eyes. They rely on other senses

Antennae 'smell' and detect vibrations

The body and its limbs are very sensitive to touch

much bigger than about 10 cm, while the smallest is a mere 5–10 mm long. Centipedes seem to move quite fast, but probably no species can leg it at more than 5 miles (8 km) per hour. The first pair of legs on a centipede are not used for walking but have been modified into poison fangs. These are used to paralyse and kill prey. Though most centipedes are harmless to human beings, there are a few foreign species now resident in Britain which can give a most unpleasant nip.

Centipedes are nocturnal. Sunlight and heat are lethal to them. Unlike insects, they do not have within their outer skin a waxy waterproof layer that retains body moisture. A few hours of exposure to dry or sunny conditions will kill a centipede. This is why you will often find dead centipedes in greenhouses or under sheets of glass. The world of the centipede is one of complete darkness. None of the British species has any form of eye. To catch their prey, centipedes rely on their highly developed sense of touch, their ability to pick up vibrations and the chemical detecting-cells in their antennae. Although most centipedes feed only on other creatures, such as woodlice, slugs, insects and smaller centipedes, there is one species at least that can damage growing celery and lettuce.

Female centipedes lay eggs one at a time. The egg is then handled by special claws at the back of the body and is smeared with a special sticky liquid to which bits of soil cling, making it hard to see. The egg is then hidden in the earth or under leaf mould and another egg is laid. From the eggs tiny but perfectly formed baby centipedes with fewer legs than the adult eventually emerge.

Keep your eyes open and you may be

able to recognize several different kinds of centipede in your garden. The *common centipede* is around 3 cm long, possesses 60 legs and holds its body rigid when running. (Most other species move with a snaky side-to-side movement.) During the day this centipede is often found beneath stones or bits of wood. Another common species, *Halophilus*, is up to 7 cm long, thin and yellowish, with 160 or more legs. *Necrophloephagus* is a yellowish centipede with a dark brown head. It is about 3.5 cm long and often burrows in gardens.

The centipede should not be confused with another multi-legged creature of the garden, the millipede. The name 'millipede' means 'a thousand feet', but no millipede has anything like that

Giant millipedes make harmless pets

Millipedes don't have a thousand legs!

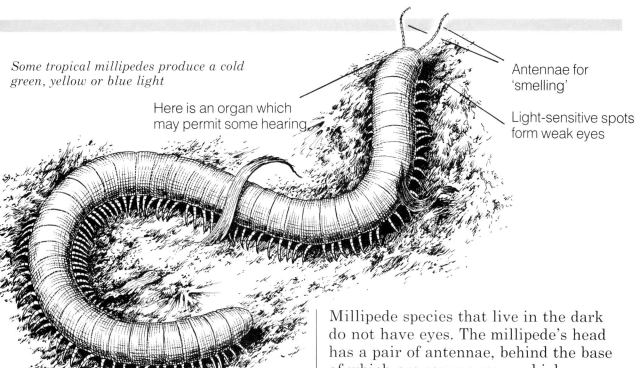

Some tropical millipedes produce a cold green, yellow or blue light

Here is an organ which may permit some hearing

Antennae for 'smelling'

Light-sensitive spots form weak eyes

number of feet! Unlike centipedes, millipedes are almost wholly vegetarian, and, whereas centipedes have one pair of legs on each segment, millipedes boast two pairs. Like centipedes, millipedes live in the soil and under leaf mould. The tiniest are only 2 mm long, but the biggest (which come from the tropics and make excellent cheap exotic pets) can reach 20 cm.

50 species of millipede live in the United Kingdom. One of the commonest is the *black snake millipede*, which grows up to 30 mm long and has 96 pairs of legs. When it is attacked it curls itself up into a flat coil so that its strong exoskeleton can protect its softer under-belly. As it rolls up it secretes a smelly poisonous liquid from a line of glands along the side of its body. This puts off most attackers. Another common British millipede is the *pill millipede* (about 50 mm long), which has a shiny body with broad back and narrow yellow bands. When threatened, it curls itself up into a little ball.

Most species of millipede have eyes, but these, unlike the powerful eyes of insects, are simply light-sensitive spots.

Millipede species that live in the dark do not have eyes. The millipede's head has a pair of antennae, behind the base of which are sense organs which may give the creature some hearing ability. Use a magnifying glass to look at the legs and movement of a millipede. The legs possess 6 or 7 joints and in most species arise close together along the middle of the under-surface. Millipedes do not move quickly but they are certainly graceful, crawling along with lovely wavy movements.

Female millipedes lay eggs from which larvae looking like miniature versions of the adults but with a smaller number of body segments and legs emerge. As the larva grows, new segments develop.

Amazingly, many foreign kinds of millipede can produce light! On the undersurface of their bodies are two kinds of glands. When mixed, the liquid secreted by these glands undergoes a remarkable chemical change, producing bluish, yellowish or greenish light. This light, which was recorded by Christopher Columbus and his companions when they visited Santo Domingo on their first voyage to the New World, has nothing to do with producing heat. It is similar to the light emitted by other kinds of living creature, such as fire-flies. It is a pity that no British variety of millipede shares this ability.

The Butterfly

Butterflies are short-lived but beautiful inhabitants of the summer garden. Despite their name, they have nothing to do with butter! The way in which the butterfly emerges from the husk that was its chrysalis or pupa is rather like something that was dead coming to life, and this is why it reminded people of the idea that when someone dies the 'soul' leaves the body and lives on. Butterflies were even thought of as the carriers of souls.

Moths are similar to butterflies and belong to the same group of insects, *Lepidoptera*; but there are some important differences between them. First, butterflies are active by day, while most moths are more active at night. Secondly, resting moths usually hold their wings spread out, while resting butterflies hold them pressed together. Thirdly, the feelers or antennae of butterflies are slender with blobs on the tips, while those of moths are short and feathery.

Butterflies are true insects and their bodies possess all the basic features of insects, with a body divided into 3 parts: head, thorax (chest) and abdomen, which has 11 rather indistinct segments. 6 legs arise from the thorax and each segment of the abdomen possesses a pair of air-tubes or spiracles opening onto the skin surface, through which the creature breathes. And, of course, they have wings. But there are many special features about butterflies which make them not only the most beautiful but also some of the cleverest creatures in your garden.

In the first place, butterflies have the keenest sense of smell in the animal kingdom. Each antenna has 40,000 tiny receptors linked to nerves for handling general smells. A male butterfly can pick up the scent of a female from as far away as 11 km, yet the total stock of perfume carried by a female is no more than 0.0001 mg! It appears that, when he has picked up the scent of a female, the male starts flying into the wind, which has carried the smell. To help him find his way, he has instruments that

The life-cycle of a butterfly

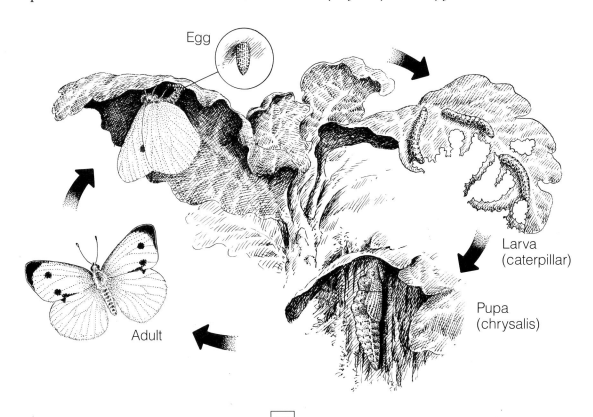

measure the wind located in joints of his antennae. So that he doesn't miss the female's scent among all the other smells in the air, the male has special receptor cells that react only to the perfume of the female.

Butterflies have 2 compound eyes, like a lot of eyes joined together. They are particularly good at receiving red colours, which is important for the pollination of plants such as the Sweet William. Unlike the human eye, the eye of the butterfly is sensitive to ultraviolet light, which allows it to see colours we can't. If a plant reflects ultraviolet light, its colour for a butterfly will be quite different from its colour for us. For instance, the red poppy reflects ultraviolet light, so to a butterfly it is not red at all but a pure ultraviolet, a sort of deep blue.

The glory of both butterflies and moths is, of course, their wings. Their family name, *Lepidoptera*, means 'scale-wings'. If you handle a butterfly gently, you will find your fingers quickly covered with a fine powder that dusts off the wings. Look at the powder under a microscope and you will see that it is made up of beautifully formed little scales. These scales are pegged to the wing like tiles on a roof. Some butterfly wings, particularly in the tropics, shimmer with blue light. This is caused by grooves on the scales, which absorb all colours in the light except blue. Butterflies are very good at flying: some species migrate, and they can travel as

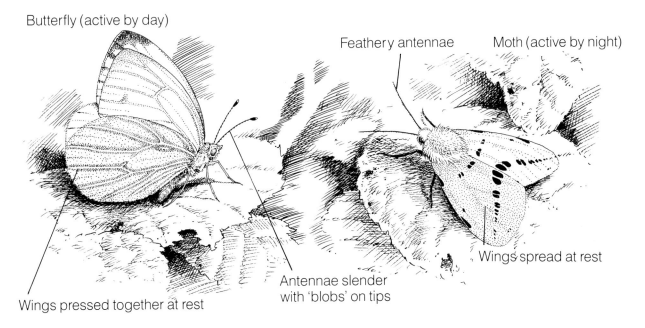

Butterfly (active by day) — Wings pressed together at rest — Antennae slender with 'blobs' on tips

Feathery antennae — Moth (active by night) — Wings spread at rest

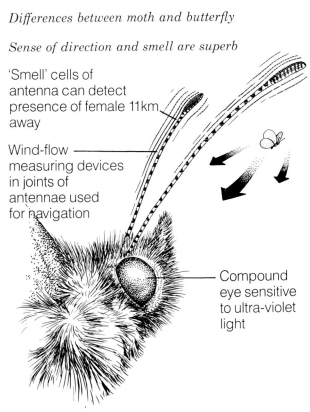

Differences between moth and butterfly

Sense of direction and smell are superb

'Smell' cells of antenna can detect presence of female 11km away

Wind-flow measuring devices in joints of antennae used for navigation

Compound eye sensitive to ultra-violet light

far as 3000 km.

Look at the head of a butterfly. At the front of the head is a 'tongue' that when not in use is coiled like a watch-spring. Actually this is a tube that when stretched right out is used to suck nectar from flowers. Almost all butterflies (and moths) feed upon nectar.

Silver studied blues

Occasionally the juices of over-ripe fruit are also taken, particularly by species such as the *red admiral*. One of Britain's rarest and most spectacular butterflies, the *purple emperor*, likes to suck the juices of the rotting bodies of animals.

If you wish to attract butterflies to your garden, you must avoid using sprays that kill insects and weeds. A bank of mixed flowers in a border is very appealing to butterflies, especially if behind it there is a brick wall that heats up in the sun. Different flowers appeal to different butterflies, so, the more varieties you have, the more different types of butterfly you are likely to see. If you can, it is a very good idea to have a patch of wild flowers.

The eggs of butterflies come in various shapes and the designs on their shells can be unbelievably beautiful, but you must look at them under a microscope to see them properly. Some females may lay a thousand or more eggs. The eggs are laid on a plant that the caterpillars can eat after they hatch. Their first meal on hatching, though, is the shell of the egg, which contains vitamins essential to the health of the caterpillars. Only one in every hundred butterfly eggs get to the point of hatching. The rest perish from disease or are eaten by birds, bugs, mites or certain flies. It usually takes 1–2 weeks for the eggs to hatch.

Caterpillars have 3 pairs of true legs attached to the thorax or chest and 5 pairs of temporary legs attached to the abdomen. The legs have hooks or claws for grasping leaves and twigs. The head has powerful cutting jaws, a pair of very short feelers or antennae, and 6 simple light-spot eyes on each side. Along the sides of the body are 9 pairs of small dots: these are breathing holes or spiracles. Beneath the mouth is an opening that leads from the glands that

The beautiful eggs of the small white

Peacock caterpillars on nettles in June

make silk, which is used to make and fix the cocoons in which the pupa or chrysalis changes into a butterfly.

Caterpillars protect themselves from enemies in a whole variety of ways. Some are hairy, some are armed with spikes and spines, and in some tropical varieties the spines are attached to poison glands and can sting. Some caterpillars protect themselves by feeding only at night; others form cases or webs on the leaves. Some hide themselves by having the same pattern or colour as the plant they feed upon. Even so, 99 per cent of caterpillars are eaten by birds and other creatures or die from disease.

As caterpillars grow, they moult their tough skins 4 times. The new skin is soft and stretches, but it soon hardens into a exoskeleton. After the fourth moult the caterpillar changes into a pupa or chrysalis. Some pupae are enclosed in a covering or cocoon of silk, while others are simply glued to a plant or hang from a silken pad. The pupa is a hard casing formed from the skin or a caterpillar with the legs glued down into it. Many sorts of chrysalis look like dead leaves or bits of dried stem, to protect them. Within the chrysalis the caterpillar gradually turns into an adult butterfly, and when it is ready the insect breaks out of the chrysalis, pumps liquid into the veins of its wings to stretch them out, and sits for up to 2 hours waiting for them to dry. Then for the first time, it soars into the air, the brand-new wings beating at up to 10 times per second.

The biggest living butterfly is the female *Queen Alexandra birdwing* of New Guinea, which has a wingspan of almost 30 cm! The biggest native British butterfly is the *swallowtail* (7–10 cm), and the smallest is the *small blue* (2–2.5 cm). If you are a real butterfly fan, the best place to go is Brazil, where there are hundreds of species, but there is still plenty of variety in Britain, with 70

The cabbage white

recorded species. Here are some of them, divided into groups by colour.

The *whites* include such species as the *small white, wood white, green-veined white* and the *orange tip*. The most familiar and notorious is the *large cabbage white*, whose caterpillars eat cabbages and other plants. There are 2 generations of large cabbage white in Britain each year, the first between April and June and the second between July and September.

There are several species of *yellow* butterfly, but the one you are most likely to see is the *brimstone*. This is a truly butter-coloured butterfly, and some people believe that it is how the butterfly got its name.

All the *brown* butterflies have false 'eye' designs on the upper or lower surfaces of their wings to deter their enemies. The commonest British butterfly is the *meadow brown*. It lives for 1 month and

The meadow brown. Note the 'eyes'

flies on dull and even rainy days. Some of the *blue* butterflies are very rare, but the one you are most likely to see in the garden is the *common blue*.

A large skipper

The brimstone butterfly

There are 8 species of British *skipper*. These are small, yellow-brownish butterflies, frequently with white markings. They are fast and quite aggressive, and will chase off other flying insects, including bees.

The gorgeous comma

The *comma* loves buddleias, asters and Michaelmas daisies. With its wings folded, the adult looks like a dead and ragged leaf.

A red admiral on buddleia flowers

The *red admiral* flies by night as well as day. It often rests and sunbathes, spreading and displaying its gorgeous wings. It delights in feeding on ice-plants, buddleias and Michaelmas daisies in the autumn.

A summer visitor: the painted lady

The *painted lady* migrates to Britain from Southern Europe and North Africa in May and June. It is very fond of garden flowers and thistles, but cannot survive the British winter.
The *fritillaries* are orange or brown butterflies with black spots. They prefer woodlands to gardens.
The *peacock* likes stinging nettles, and you should look for its black, hairy caterpillars on these plants in June. The adult enjoys feeding on the sap of ripe fruit in orchards. It gets its name from the eyes on its wings, which are intended to 'stare' at and frighten away enemies.

The glamorous peacock butterfly

The Bee

The bee is the royal emblem of France. Yes, it is true that the emblem is called the fleur-de-lis, which is French for the iris, but this shape was originally meant to represent a flying bee. The old royal robe and banners of France were thickly sewn

The fleur-de-lis: not a plant, but a bee

with golden bees, and when the tomb of the early French king Childeric (436–81 AD) was opened in the seventeenth century it was found to contain 300 bees made of gold.

People like bees because they make honey and pollinate flowers. Everybody knows that they are very busy creatures, and you will often see them working in your garden. Some species, such as the *honey bee*, live in well-organized colonies or hives. These bees are called 'social' bees, and the females are of 2 types: there are a few 'queen' bees, who can lay eggs, and lots and lots of 'worker' bees, who cannot breed at all. The males are called 'drones'. You may be surprised to learn that most species of bee are 'solitary' bees: they live on their own, and the female makes a nest for her 'brood', the larvae that hatch from the eggs she lays.

Bees are insects and have hairy, plump bodies which are large compared with their wings. The joints of the hind legs are specially big and covered with thick hair, which collects pollen. The eggs of bees are laid singly in chambers or cells, and each bee's nest contains a number of cells; the hive bee's has many thousands. Along with each egg enough food is deposited to feed the larva until it turns into a pupa. Adult bees feed on nectar and pollen from flowers. The larvae also eat pollen and honey, which is made from nectar in the bee's 'honey

The body of the bee

stomach' and then brought up again at the nest or hive. Honey is a form of concentrated nectar rich in sugars. Pollen contains lots of protein.

Solitary bees make their nests in a variety of places. Some make burrows in the ground, with single cells leading off a main passage. Others make use of spaces they find in buildings, walls, trees or bushes. They may even use keyholes or empty snail shells!

Honey bees build the cells of the hive out of scales of wax, which they produce from glands on the under-surface of their abdomens. They shape the wax by lifting it on their legs and kneading it with their jaws. To seal cracks in the honeycomb, bees like to collect resin from trees. If there are no trees available, they may fetch warm tar from a nearby road. To soften the wax of the honeycomb, water is needed, and every day some bees will go in search of ponds and puddles. The cells are built very carefully. The bee measures everything it does using its antennae and the sensitive bristles on its abdomen. If the honeycomb is damaged, the bees at once start making repairs.

The bee that you see in the garden is a living machine far more complex than

A typical beehive

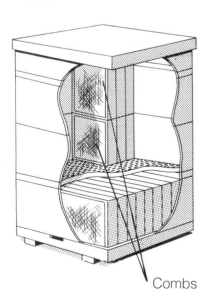
Combs

any rocket or computer. Bees have a perfect sense of temperature and can detect rises or falls of less than 1°C. Temperature control is very important to honey bees, and they have worked out ways of keeping a constant temperature of 35°C in the hive's

A bee-keeper inspects a honeycomb

breeding-cells. In cool weather, worker bees crowd together in their thousands on top of the cells to warm them up. If it goes colder, they huddle closer and cover the brood cells with their bodies to make a living eiderdown. On the other hand, if it is too hot they bring in water and cover the combs with a fine film which they then cause to evaporate by fanning it with their wings. They sit like little ventilators over the cells driving the warm air towards each other and pushing it out again through the entrance.

The compound eye of the bee is made up of 15,000 parts or facets, which are like lots of separate eyes and divide everything the bee sees into a screen of squares. It uses this screen in order to find its way and work out its speed. As the bee flies along, it charts its course in relation to the sun and the way in which what it sees changes on its screen and so tells how fast it is flying.

The bee also has a mechanism that works out air-speed. This is centred in nerves within the joints of the antennae. When the wind bends the antennae, signals are sent into the central computer. By comparing the signals from the antennae with the information from the eye about the bee's flying-speed, the computer works out at once the angle at which the bee should fly. What is more, the eyeball of a bee has rows of tiny hairs where the facets join. These hairs sense air-movements, and in next to no time the bee can correct its flight when it is affected by gusts of wind, so that it is not blown off-course.

In the hairy fur between the bee's compound eyes are 3 tiny eye spots, which are used to measure how light it is (like the lightmeter on a camera). These light meters are very important, because they tell a bee when it is safe to go out in the morning and also when it should return home. The bee's computer tells it how far it is from the hive or nest, and as the light fades the bee can tell when it must leave for home and how fast it must fly to reach there at the right time.

The bee's two antennae have nerve receptors which react to the level of carbon dioxide in the air. If the amount rises, it immediately triggers off a rapid fanning motion of the wings. This mechanism is employed by worker bees to ensure that the air in the hive is always fresh. The chemical receptors of the antennae can also pick up the scents of blossoms, and, depending on which antenna picks up the stronger scent, the bee knows which way to fly to find the flowers producing the scent. (If

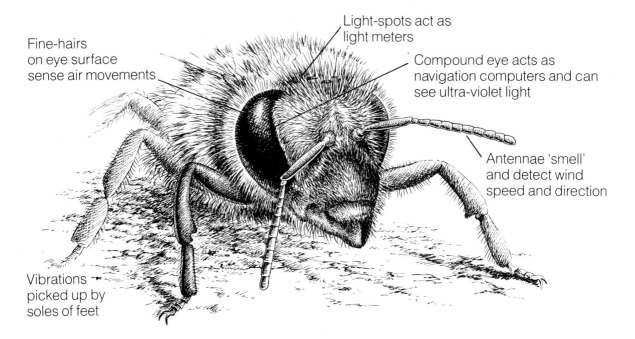

A bee's senses are truly amazing

both antennae give the same message, the bee is heading in the right direction.) The antennae are not the only way in which bees seek out food flowers. They use their eyes too, and because they (like butterflies) can see ultra-violet light, they see things in a completely different way from us. One colour they cannot see is red, which looks black to them. But, because some flowers that look red to us reflect ultra-violet light, the bee sees them as a deep blue!

Bees cannot hear in the same way as we can, but they can pick up vibrations through the soles of their feet and use vibrations to 'speak' to other bees.

Bees swarming on a tree trunk

Another way in which bees can communicate with each other is through dancing! The other bees watch the dance and get the message at once.

You may one day see bees swarm in your garden. This happens when there are too many bees in a colony. The colony prepares to divide by swarming. Dense balls containing thousands of bees form a swarm and they tend to occur between May and July. You might see them attached to the branch of a tree as a sort of buzzing ball, and sometimes they will build a temporary honeycomb there before setting up the new colony. If bees do swarm in your garden, don't be frightened but leave the bees alone. You should ask a local beekeeper for advice. He may move the swarm, which has to be done very carefully.

Despite all their skills and industry, most bees do not live very long. Honey bees live for only about 1 month in summer. Lots of people think that all the bees they see in the garden are honey bees, but in fact there are over 200 different species of bee in Britain and the honey bee is only one of them. *Bumble bees*, of which there are 18

The same flower visited by a bumble bee

A honey bee at work

species in Britain, are easily recognized because of their big furry bodies. Like honey bees, they are social bees. Each colony has one queen, plus lots of female workers and male drones.

Everyone knows that bees can sting. The sting is a sort of poison needle that sticks out from the end of the abdomen. Worker bees use it as a means of defence and always die after stinging, as the sting is barbed (like an arrow) and cannot be pulled out when it has been used. Queen bees that have not bred and laid eggs have unbarbed stings, used for killing other queens.

The Frog

To me frogs and toads are fascinating animals. They are quiet, neat, slightly comical creatures and they live in ponds. You often see frogs in your garden, even if there is no pond or pool but just some damp and shady areas.

Frogs are amphibians – creatures that live both on land and in water – but unlike reptiles (such as snakes) they have naked, moist skin which is used in breathing to obtain oxygen. Most young amphibians hatch from eggs that are deposited in water and develop into larvae that breath through external gills in a similar way to fish. They gradually change into animals that can live on land. Their gills disappear and they begin to breathe through their skin and a brand-new pair of lungs.

There are 1800 species of frog and

The common toad

A frog at home

toad in the world today. The biggest frog in the world is the rare *Goliath frog* from Guinea in West Africa. The biggest frog in Britain is the *marsh frog*, which arrived from Hungary in 1935. From the tip of its nose to the base of its rump it measures 10–13 cm, while the biggest native frog, the *common frog*, doesn't quite reach 10 cm.

Although some toads are long-lived and can perhaps reach 40 years of age, frogs tend not to live anywhere near as long. There may be exceptions (we don't know much about the Goliath frog, for instance), but the limit for the species we know a lot about seems to be about 16 years.

If you pick up a frog, hold it very gently and look at it carefully. Don't keep it in your warm hands for more than a minute or two – such a cool and damp-skinned animal finds it most uncomfortable! The frog has a special kind of tongue which is fixed to the front of the mouth and can be flicked forward. Within the tongue are lots of glands which ooze and make it sticky. When a frog sees an insect, it flicks out its tongue, which sticks to the insect and pulls it back into the frog's mouth. Although adult frogs are carnivores, their larvae (tadpoles) are vegetarians when first hatched and feed on algae, which are tiny plants that grow in water.

Watch a frog sitting quietly, gulping from time to time as its throat pumps up and down. What it is doing is breathing

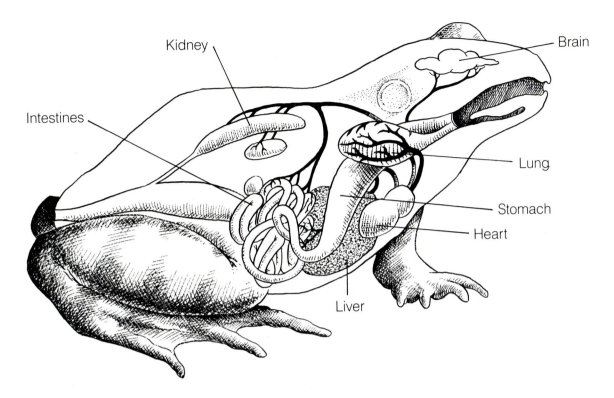

The basic body plan of a frog

by swallowing air and squeezing it down into its lungs. As frogs have almost no ribs and no diaphragm (the muscle between chest and abdomen), they can't breathe with their chests.

Frogs have a larynx or voice-box at the top of their windpipe. This is what they use to croak. Some frogs, such as the *edible frog* of continental Europe, have pouches on the sides of their throat which they can blow out to make their croaking louder. Breathing through the skin is even more important for frogs than breathing through their lungs, which they cannot use when hibernating under water.

The eyes of a frog are well developed and have tear-glands and eyelids that close. It has been discovered that usually their eyes do not pick out anything that is not moving. They are programmed, however, to react to blue and green. When they are threatened, blue means water and safety, while green means grass and spells danger. This means that when they are frightened they will even jump at a piece of blue paper, thinking that it is water. Frogs' eyes bulge and make room when a large object is swallowed, as there is no bone between the roof of the mouth and the eye-socket, just thin sheets of soft tissue.

Frogs hear well and their ears are very sensitive to ground vibrations, which are transmitted through the

Frogs can't 'see' anything that doesn't move

forelegs and shoulders. Amphibians are very sensitive to smells in the air and like snakes have the so-called 'Jacobsen's organ', which enables them to tell what is the air by flicking out their tongue.

Frogs are very good at jumping. The record is held by the South African *sharp-nosed frog*, which has been known to cover almost 10 m in three leaps. It is said that this frog can jump 4.57 m in a single leap.

In spring, frogs go back to the pond or pool where they were born. The amount of daylight, and the temperature of the moisture in the air tell them when to move, and they may travel up to 3 km to reach their home pond. Frogs are very clever at finding their way: they recognize landmarks, and some species can tell where to go from the position of the sun and stars. In autumn they move from their summer haunts to their hibernation sites, which are often the same pond.

During mating, all the senses of the frog come into play. They are attracted by sounds (mating-calls), smells and sight, as well as touch. Male frogs have highly sensitive 'pimples' on their breasts and toes, and females have similar tiny points on their backs. These are stimulated when they are touched. The skin-colour of a frog can change gradually according to where it lives. This change is controlled by a gland in the brain (the pituitary gland), the same one as tells the frog when it is time to go home to mate.

Each species of frog has its own particular voice, and frogs croak and call for a variety of reasons. Male do so to show off during the mating-season and attract females, or to declare

Some frogs can jump over 4½ m

ownership of territory. Distressed and alarmed frogs often cry out, and the delightful, vividly coloured *tree frogs* of the tropics croak for joy when rain falls!

The frog you are most likely to find in your garden is the *common* or *grass frog*, particularly on damp days or at night. This animal has a yellow to greenish-

Frogs mating on Hampstead Heath

brown skin with numerous blotches and stripes and dark markings. Look at the eyes and see how they are set high on the head – perfect for peeping cautiously out of the water. Notice that the pupils in the eyes run from side to side. The common frog tends to live alone outside the mating-season. The female lays 1000–4000 eggs in a large clump of frogspawn. After the eggs have been deposited in the water they are fertilized by the male, so that they can produce tadpoles.

It is a good thing that female frogs lay so many eggs: most of them never develop into adult frogs. The enemies of the frog are many, and include snakes, mammals such as foxes, otters, hedgehogs and rats, fish such as the pike and perch, and birds such as herons, hawks, seagulls, ducks and geese. Added to this, frogs are attacked by many diseases and parasites (creatures that live on or inside other animals). The frog's greatest enemy, though, is man, who especially over the last 20 years has drained and filled in many ponds and ditches, places where frogs used to live but now cannot. The water in many ponds has been polluted, and the use of insecticides (chemical sprays and the like designed to kill insects) cuts down frogs' food-supply and can cause other damage.

If you want to help the frog, keep your garden pond clean and make sure it is not choked with weeds. Have lots of plants growing round the edge to

Frogs are amphibians not reptiles

provide shade and shelter. Use insecticides as little as possible, and, if you do collect frogspawn in the spring to watch it hatch into tadpoles and see how the tadpoles change into frogs, please make sure that, as soon as the little creatures have grown their hind legs, you release them into the pond or lake where you found the frogspawn.

The Snail

All that most people know about snails is that they move very slowly and that they can be pests in the garden. There is much more than that to them, however. Some are still well under 1 mm long when fully grown, but they are relatives of the octopus, the pearl oyster and the monster giant squid, which grows to a size of 20 m across and battles with sperm whales 5000 m down in the ocean depths. Snails in times gone by were often cruelly treated, particularly in the preparation of folk medicines and charms. Some country people used to think that if they swallowed snails it would stop them coughing!

Snails are members of the group of animals called molluscs, which includes 60,000 species. Molluscs are such

The humble snail is related to the octopus

Snails are molluscs, soft-bodied animals that make mobile homes of shell

Shell made of chalk with a little protein

successful creatures that they are found nearly everywhere, on land and in water. They have many different designs. Most belong to a sub-group called *Gastropoda*, and, although many have shells protecting their soft bodies, others, such as slugs, do not.

A snail's body consists of a head that can be moved very easily and is packed with sense organs. Behind the head are the internal organs (heart, liver, intestines, and so on) surrounded by a covering of soft tissue. The upper part of this covering is called the 'mantle' and hangs down round the body to enclose a hollow with a damp lining that acts as the lungs and absorbs oxygen for breathing. The lower part of the soft covering is enlarged into a muscular foot which contains a mouth fitted with rows of horny teeth (the 'radula'). This curious design, which allows the snail to gnaw its food with its foot, explains the Latin name *Gastropoda*, which means 'stomach feet'. A snail's blood is not red but colourless and circulates through blood-vessels pumped by a heart with 3 chambers.

The shell is made up of chemicals secreted by the mantle. It is made up of a small amount of a kind of protein mixed with a large amount of chalk. Because the snail needs a source of chalky chemicals, you will not find many snails on acid soils.

The biggest land-snail is the *giant African snail* (which makes a most interesting and cheap pet for a keen young biologist). Its body may be over 20 cm long, and it can weigh as much as 250 gm. The Japanese army brought this snail to the Pacific area during the Second World War as a source of fresh food. At the end of the war the American troops accidentally imported the species into the United States.

A pest: the giant African snail

Because the giant African breeds very quickly and is very destructive, it soon became a problem in farming areas. It has been estimated that one snail can produce around 11 million offspring over a period of 5 years. Attempts have been made to control the vegetarian giant African snail by introducing species of carnivorous snails which prey upon it.

There are 80 species of land-snail in Britain, of which the biggest is the *Roman* or *edible snail*, which occurs in limestone areas in the south and is rather rare. Its body is up to 10 cm long and it weighs up to 90 gm. This snail was introduced by the Romans as food, and has a strong, round, creamy-coloured shell. The *common garden snail* has a round shell that is pale brown with up to 5 dark bands and measures about 35 mm across. Like most snails, it is active mainly at night. During the day it retreats to its favourite damp spot and has a nap. In the winter or if the weather is unusually hot and dry, snails seal up the opening of their shell with a thick sticky film to save the moisture inside.

Snails are 'hermaphrodites', which means that they are not male or female but *both*, so they can *all* lay eggs. However, they still have to mate. During mating, which usually occurs at night in summer, they come together and stab one another with a tiny barbed arrow made of chalk. This injects spermatozoa, living male organisms which then set about fertilizing the female eggs contained within each snail. The eggs, which are tiny and white, are laid in batches of up to 40 in holes in the soil. After 4 weeks or so, perfect mini-snails emerge.

Other land-snails which you may come across in the garden include the *moss snail*, which has a light brown body and a long cone-shaped shell around 6 mm long that is shiny and pale to dark-brown in colour. This snail loves damp moss, piles of dead leaves and compost-heaps. The *tree snail* has a long, cone-shaped, brownish or greenish shell about 10 mm long, and may be seen on treetrunks or dry stone walls in gardens. The *white-lipped banded snail* has a shiny, thin, round shell about 17 mm wide and 20 mm high, slightly flattened on the sides. The shell-colour varies, but is often yellow, with up to 5 dark bands. The snail's body is greenish-grey. The *dark-lipped banded snail* has a much thicker and more rounded shell about 22 mm wide and 25 mm high; the colour varies from yellow to brown and the number of bands varies too. The body is greyish-yellow. The colours and markings of banded snails' shells depend on where the snails live, helping them blend into their surroundings more easily. They are darker in woodland than in gardens because woodland colours are darker than garden colours. My favourite garden snail is the tiny (5 mm high and wide) *garlic glass snail*,

One of the snail's great enemies, the thrush

emits a strong smell of garlic if upset or handled.

Snails can live for up to 10 years, but they have lots of enemies. The most famous is the thrush, which uses a stone to crack open their shells and eat their soft bodies.

A snail 'family snapshot'

HISTORY IN DEPTH

INDIA, FROM THE RAJ TO INDEPENDENCE

Sydney Wood

MACMILLAN

© Sydney Wood 1989

All rights reserved. No reproduction, copy or transmission
of this publication may be made without written permission.

No paragraph of this publication may be reproduced, copied
or transmitted save with written permission or in accordance
with the provisions of the Copyright Act 1956 (as amended),
or under the terms of any licence permitting limited copying
issued by the Copyright Licensing Agency, 33–4 Alfred Place,
London WC1E 7DP.

Any person who does any unauthorised act in relation to
this publication may be liable to criminal prosecution and
civil claims for damages.

First published 1989

Published by
MACMILLAN EDUCATION LTD
Houndmills, Basingstoke, Hampshire RG21 2XS
and London
Companies and representatives
throughout the world

Printed in Hong Kong

British Library Cataloguing in Publication Data
Wood, Sydney
India: from the Raj to independence. ——
(History in depth).
1. India. Political events, 1858–1947
I. Title   II. Series
954.03′5
ISBN 0–333–46356–0

CONTENTS

	Preface	4
1	The Raj	5
2	Amritsar	17
3	Gandhi and the Congress Party	26
4	Jinnah and the Muslim League	38
5	Crisis, 1939–46	46
6	The end of British India	52
	Index	64

Acknowledgements

The author and publishers wish to acknowledge, with thanks, the following photographic sources:

BBC Hulton Picture Library pp14 top, 28, 31 top, 31 centre, 34 top, 41, 44, 45, 55, 58 top; British Museum in India, Colne, Lancs p9, copyright reserved, reproduced by gracious permission of Her Majesty the Queen; Ronald Grant Archive pp17 top, 17 bottom; *Illustrated London News* p23; Harald Lechenperg p14 bottom; Mansell Collection p36; William McQuitty pp16, 31 bottom; National Army Museum p22; Photo Source pp46, 49 top, 49 bottom, 53; Popperfoto pp6 bottom, 8, 11, 12, 15 top, 30, 34 bottom, 43, 52, 54, 58 bottom, 60; Sole Syndication and Literary Agency Ltd. p19.

The publishers have made every effort to trace all the copyright holders, but if any have been inadvertently overlooked, they will be pleased to make the necessary arrangements at the first opportunity.

PREFACE

The study of history is exciting, whether in a good story well told, a mystery solved by the judicious unravelling of clues, or a study of the men, women and children whose fears and ambitions, successes and tragedies make up the collective memory of mankind.

This series aims to reveal this excitement to pupils through a set of topic books on important historical subjects from the Middle Ages to the present day. Each book contains four main elements: a narrative and descriptive text, lively and relevant illustrations, extracts of contemporary evidence, and questions for further thought and work. Involvement in these elements should provide an adventure which will bring the past to life in the imagination of the pupil.

Each book is also designed to develop the knowledge, skills and concepts so essential to a pupil's growth. It provides a wide, varying introduction to the evidence available on each topic. In handling this evidence, pupils will increase their understanding of basic historical concepts such as causation and change, as well as of more advanced ideas such as revolution and democracy. In addition, their use of basic study skills will be complemented by more sophisticated historical skills such as the detection of bias and the formulation of opinion.

The intended audience for the series is pupils of eleven to sixteen years; it is expected that the earlier topics will be introduced in the first three years of secondary school, while the nineteenth and twentieth century topics are directed towards first examinations.

1 THE RAJ

The Indian princely states

What do you think it would be like to be at a cricket match where the captain of one of the sides behaved like this:

Maharajah: prince

> At three o'clock in the afternoon the Maharajah would come down to the ground, the band would play the Kashmir anthem, and he then went off to a special tent where he sat for a time, smoking his long waterpipe. At four thirty he decided he would bat. It didn't matter which side was batting, his own team or ours. He was padded by two attendants and gloved by two more, somebody carried his bat and he walked out to the wicket looking very dignified, very small and with an enormous turban on his head. In one of the matches I happened to be bowling and my first ball hit his stumps, but the wicket keeper, quick as lightning, shouted 'No Ball!' and the match went on. The only way that the Maharajah could get out was by l.b.w. And after fifteen or twenty minutes batting he said he felt tired and he was duly given out l.b.w. What the scorers did about his innings, which was never less than half a century, goodness only knows.
>
> C. Allen: *Plain Tales from the Raj*, 1975

This maharajah ruled a large state in India during the early twentieth century. Why do you think he was allowed to behave like this?

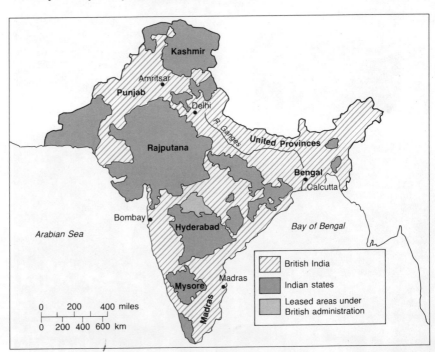

India in the 1900s. 61.5 per cent of the country was ruled by British administrators. The rest consisted of 601 separate states ruled by Indian princes. Some were huge – Hyderabad was bigger than England and Wales – but others were tiny.

Using the evidence

The following sources deal with different aspects of princely rule in the 1900s.

A In 1900 the head of the British Government in India, the Viceroy, was Lord Curzon. He described the princes as:

> ...unruly and ignorant and rather undisciplined schoolboys. What they want more than anything else is to be schooled by a firm hand. We sustain the Native States and Princes not so much in the interests of the Princes themselves, who are often quite undeserving, as in the interests of the people, who are supposed to like the old traditions and dynasties and rule. But supposing we allow Native India to be governed by a horde of frivolous absentees who have lost the respect and affection of their own subjects — what justification shall we have for maintaining the Native States at all? No, we are bound to train and discipline, and control them, and so to fit them for the unique position which we have placed within their grasp. They are beginning to see that Princes cannot afford to live exclusively in palaces, but that they must be out and about, setting an example among their fellow-creatures.
>
> Quoted in C.H. Philips' book, *The Evolution of India and Pakistan*, 1962

B

The ruler, or 'Nawab', of Bahawalpur in 1903. His richly embroidered coat and necklace of exceptionally large rubies show his wealth.

C

Celebrations in an Indian state where a new maharajah has succeeded to the throne. The elephant carries the senior British official in the state to the palace. How does this scene show the importance of the Raj even in princely states?

D Indian princes were often sent to Britain for their education. The ruler of Dhrangadhara observed:

Whether you were educated in India or abroad, the point was really how far you went in adopting alien ways and rejecting your own, in clothes, or ballroom dancing, or your language. Anglicisation brought you closer to the British overlords, which in those days was a matter of great importance. There is no greater flattery than imitation. But when it took away your native fervour, others, quite naturally, filled the place.
Quoted in C. Allen's book, *The Lives of the Indian Princes*, 1984

E Indian princes and their families enjoyed power, wealth and privilege. The only child of the ruler of Idar recalled:

Everywhere you went you were the centre of attraction and everyone fawned over you. You always had people hovering around you trying to see that you never hurt yourself, trying to see that you never fell sick. It was more like being wrapped up in silk rather than cotton wool. You thought the whole world was rosy; I mean you never came across anything sad or anything bad. Till I was twelve I had never even heard of poverty and I never saw poverty. Even people who were working as servants in the palaces, you never thought of them as being poor. They were all in their uniforms, and they were all spick and span.
Quoted in C. Allen's book, as above

1 What evidence can you find in the sources to show British power over the maharajahs?

2 a) Lord Curzon was a very forceful and dominant Viceroy. What does source **A** imply was his attitude to Indian people and society?
   b) Do you think source **A** gives a complete picture of what the Indian princes were like? What other sources might you try to find, to see if Indian princes were really 'ignorant and rather undisciplined schoolboys'?

3 a) Which source suggests that, for some princes, British influence weakened their importance in their states?
   b) What danger is hinted at in this source?

4 How well prepared for power might a ruler be who was brought up like the person in source **E**? Explain your answer.

5 Which of the above sources would be most useful to someone investigating princely rule? Explain your answer.

The Viceroy's Palace in New Delhi. The splendour of the building shows the importance of the head of British government in India.

British India

British officials directly ruled most of India, and ever since 1858 its laws had been made by the British Parliament in Westminster. However, such was the distance between the two countries that a great many decisions had to be left to the men on the spot. British judges, British army officers and British police officers were involved in controlling India. Indians served as policemen, as lawyers, and as soldiers (there were more than 100 000 men in the Indian Army in peacetime); but there were always British officers and officials above them. Most of all, power lay with the members of the Indian Civil Service (ICS), who were responsible for administering India, settling disputes and encouraging economic development. Contemporaries differed in their judgment of the ICS.

Using the evidence

A Stanley Reed was a British journalist in early-twentieth-century India. This is how it appeared to him:

...a country as large as Europe without Russia, peopled by a quarter of the human race, heirs to an ancient and great civilization, a mixture of race and creed separated by many languages; yet the effective administration was in the hands of a corps d'elite, never more than a thousand strong, backed by a British Army of fifty thousand or so. Behind this stood the specialized services Forests and Public Works, Police and so forth; but power and authority, save for the shadowy control of a remote Parliament, lay with the Civil Service.

S. Reed: *The India I Knew*, 1952

corps d'elite: group of special people

B   The Viceroy, Lord Curzon, believed:

There are neither originality, nor ideas, nor imagination in the Indian Civil Service; they think the present the best, and improvement or reform sends a cold shiver down their spine. Where would have been any one of the great subjects that I have taken up – Education, Irrigation, Police, Railways – if I had waited for the Local Governments to give the cue?
Quoted in C.H. Philips' book, *The Evolution of India and Pakistan*, 1962

C   A few Indians entered the ICS. One of them, Rajeshwar Dayal, thought the aim was to recruit:

... good, all-round people who could get on horseback and ride round the country, meting out rough and ready justice. They were looking for the sort of qualities that they favoured in their public schools. They expected people to be reliable chaps who could face a riotous mob or deal with a flood situation.
Quoted in Z. Masani's book, *Indian Tales of the Raj*, 1987

D
An ICS officer at work. Much time was spent settling disputes. Members of the ICS were well paid and were expected to resist the bribes they were offered.

E   Entry to the ICS was by examination. It attracted applications from Indians educated at one of the seven universities or at the many colleges that had been set up by the British in India. In 1919, for the first time, the exams were held in Delhi and Rangoon as well as in Britain. In 1923 the Lee Commission decided that by 1938 half the ICS officials should be Indian. Before 1919 it was very hard for Indians to enter the ICS. Stanley Reed explained:

There was nothing on paper to stop the Indian from competing in the Civil Service examinations, but to do so he had to sit [the exams] in London and round off his education at a British university. He or his family had to find the ready cash, certainly not less than £1,000. The candidate had to face the risks of higher education in a foreign country and a severe test in unfamiliar surroundings. A limited number of Indians won through, and some attained high office. So serious was this handicap that in a personnel of twelve hundred in the early part of this century not more than fifty were natives.

S. Reed: *The India I Knew*, 1952

F In 1900, Lord Curzon complained:

An increasing number of the higher posts that were meant, and ought to have been exclusively and specially reserved, for Europeans, are being filched away by the superior wits of the native in the English examinations. I believe it to be the greatest peril with which our administration is confronted.

Quoted in B.N. Pandey's book, *The Breakup of British India*, 1969

1 Using the evidence provided, explain the meaning of 'Civil Service'. What would you say were the main duties of ICS officials?

2 Sources **A** and **B** were both written by British people, yet they differ greatly. What are the main differences between them? How would you account for these differences?

3 a) What do you think was the main reason for the small number of Indian ICS officials?
   b) Why do you think Lord Curzon thought that Indian entry was a great peril?

Indian society

In the 1900s, around 100 000 British people lived in India. The country's total population was vast — 303 million in 1911 — so many Indians rarely saw a white person. The country exported raw cotton, jute, tea and coffee. Its various industries, in particular iron, cotton, jute and coal, were quite small, and even in 1939 there were only two million industrial workers. According to one Indian:

Basically the British were interested in that kind of industrial growth which would help them back in Britain. They needed hessian — so

Summer Hill station, Simla. During the very hot season British officials moved to Simla and other hilly places where the heat was less intense.

they developed jute. They needed the railways to transport the raw materials to the coastal areas.

Dr Ashak Mitra, quoted in Z. Masani's book, *Indian Tales of the Raj*, 1987

Questions

1 Explain the meaning of 'industrial growth'.

2 Dr Mitra was an expert economist. He was also opposed to British rule. Do you think it is safe to accept the view he is offering? Give reasons for your answer.

Only a small percentage of Indians earned a living from industry. The British developed roads, railways, bridges, canals, postal services and irrigation schemes; yet for most Indians life went on much as it had done for many decades, little touched by all these changes. A large population that depended so much on farming could suffer heavily if something went wrong. Stanley Reed noted:

The rains failed in 1896 and 1899. The actual deaths from hunger were placed at about a million. But what no government could entirely control was the fearful sweep of cholera in the relief camps, and the toll of malaria. Plague baffled all measures. On top of these misfortunes was the devastating epidemic of influenza in 1918, which caused twelve million deaths.

...At the little city of Udaipur, in the hot weather of 1900, the deaths from cholera were four hundred a day; the bulk of the inhabitants drew their water from one contaminated source. In the same month, at Godhra, fifteen hundred men and women perished from cholera in three days, and the dead were borne to the burning-ground in cart-loads.

S. Reed: *The India I Knew*, 1952

The family who lived in this house were members of the lowest caste of Indian Hindu society, the 'untouchables'. Note the size of the house and the materials used to build it.

The people who inhabited this vast land spoke many different languages. A tiny minority of Indians, from the wealthy classes, attended schools set up by British missionaries and churches, where they learned English. But in 1900 three out of four villages still had no school of any sort. The country's 186 colleges were attended by a mere 36 000 Indian students. Many different religious faiths flourished in India, too. Most people – around 70 per cent of the population – were Hindus. But a significant minority – about 21 per cent – followed the Muslim faith. There were also sizeable numbers of Sikhs and Christians.

Question

'No individual could do much to change India.' What points in the above paragraph suggest that this might be true? Do you think it is likely to be true?

Attitudes in the Raj

Some British people who came to India sought profit or adventure. Others would have supported the views of Lord Curzon:

If I thought it were all for nothing, and that Englishmen, Scotchmen and Irishmen in this country were simply writing inscriptions on the sand to be washed out by the next tide; if I felt that we were not working here for the good of India in obedience to a higher law and a nobler aim, then I would see the link that holds England and India together severed without a sigh. But it is because I believe in the future of this country and the capacity of our own race to guide it to goals that it has never hitherto attained, that I keep courage and press forward.

Quoted in D. Judd's book, *The British Raj*, 1972

A column of British troops marching along the North-West Frontier. A third of the soldiers in the Indian Army were British and were organised in separate regiments.

The Raj — the British rulers of India — tended to take their Empire for granted. When Britain declared war on Germany in 1914, India was automatically drawn in and Indian troops were sent to fight in British campaigns.

> *Within six months of the outbreak of the war eighty thousand British officers and troops and two hundred and ten thousand Indian officers and men were sent overseas. The Indian Princes placed all their resources at the disposal of the King; the Indian community donated great sums to the Red Cross; the Indian factories produced tents, boots, saddlery and clothing; the arsenals and the stores [produced] rifles, cannon and small-arms ammunition. India was the reservoir for the manpower which made final victory possible.*
>
> S. Reed: *The India I Knew*, 1952

Indian pupils at schools run by the British often found themselves wearing British-style uniforms, learning British games, and studying textbooks produced in Britain. An Indian who went to one of these schools remembers:

prescribed: ordered to be used

imperialist: stressing the importance of the Empire

> *The school textbooks prescribed in British days had a strong imperialist flavour. I remember how many of us squirmed on being called upon to recite a poem about an English hero who was killed in a frontier skirmish:*
> 'Let dusky Indians whine and kneel,
> An English lad must die.'
> *I forget who was the author of this sensitive piece.*
>
> Frank Moraes: *Witness to an Era*, 1973

Although there were British people who developed a love of and respect for Indian culture and society, many behaved like John Morris, an army officer, who recalled that in 1916:

> *I went on to the train in Bombay and discovered that the other berth was occupied by an Indian. I am sorry to say that by that time I*

A late-nineteenth-century picture of a British officer being attended by Indian servants.

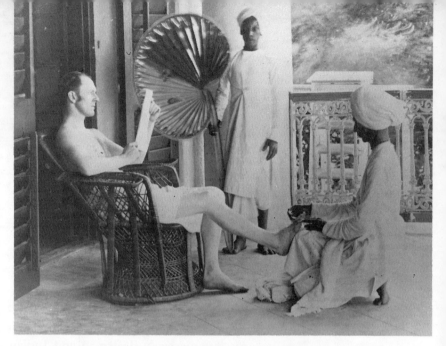

had become affected by the mentality of the ruling class in India and I said to the stationmaster, 'I want to have the gentleman ejected.' He spoke absolutely perfect English and he could have taught me a great deal about India. It is one of the incidents of my life of which I am most ashamed. But you have to remember that in those days army officers did not associate with Indians of any class other than the servant class, to whom they just gave orders. I think that one of the chief reasons for the curious attitude of the British towards Indians — it may have been quite unconscious — was the fact that they were regarded as a subject race.

a subject race: a group ruled by another group

Quoted in C. Allen's book, *Plain Tales from the Raj*, 1975

In 1869 the opening of the Suez Canal made the journey from Europe to India much shorter. This encouraged many British girls to go to India in search of husbands, and the ships on which they

This Indian's job was to work a fan to move the air in an oven-hot living-room. A man doing such a job was called a 'punkah wallah'. Would you agree with the view that 'an Indian would be glad to do work like this'?

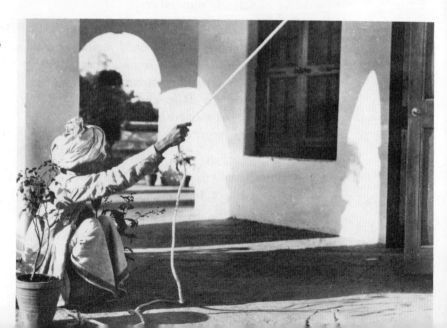

travelled came to be known as 'the fishing fleet'. Vera Birdwood, who lived in India, thought that many British women were even more cut off from Indian society than the men were:

We were looked after by Indian servants and we met a great many Indians, and some of us undoubtedly made a very close study of India and Indian customs, but once you stepped inside the home you were back in Cheltenham or Bath. We brought with us in our home lives almost exact replicas of the sort of life that upper-middle-class people lived in England at that time. Nearly everyone in official India sprang from precisely the same educational and cultural background. You went from bungalow to bungalow and you found the same sort of furniture, the same sort of dinner table set, the same kind of conversation. We read the same books, mostly imported by post from England, and I can't really say that we took an awful lot from India.

Quoted in C. Allen's book, as above

Above: the Calcutta Golf Club, photographed in 1910. What evidence in the picture would help you to work out that it came from this period?

Right: Peshawar in 1905. During the twentieth century the population in India's towns has grown rapidly. What evidence would you select from this picture to prove that this is not a British town?

A buffalo cart, 1927. What do you think the driver's feelings might have been towards his European passengers?

It is not surprising that some Indians reacted to the Raj like this:

> *I was influenced by the example of my parents who never went into any kind of society in which they were not treated as equals. I entertained no ambition whatever of hobnobbing with the English in India. As long as I lived in Calcutta I wore no article of English clothing and had none. In general, I disliked and despised the local English.*
>
> Nirad Chaudhuri: *The Autobiography of an Unknown Indian*, 1951

However, in the early years of the twentieth century, forces were at work that were to transform life in India and bring to an end the British Raj which, in 1900, had seemed so unshakeably strong.

Questions

1. List as many reasons as possible that explain why Britain wished to have control over India.

2. a) What were the main differences between a British-controlled state and a princely state?
   b) Which do you think an ordinary Indian of the time might have preferred to live in?

3. How would you account for the fact that a small number of British people were able to rule so vast an area as India?

4. What do you think Vera Birdwood meant by 'cultural background'?

5. Does any of the evidence in this chapter suggest that the behaviour of the British might lead to trouble for the Raj?

2 AMRITSAR

The massacre

Imagine you are part of a large crowd of 15 000 or more people who have gathered in your city's main meeting place. It is late afternoon. Some people are eating and drinking. Some are chatting. Many are listening to speeches. Nobody is fighting or carrying weapons. Shouts from some of the people draw your attention to the entrance to the meeting place. Soldiers have marched in and are lining up and aiming rifles at the crowd. There is a command from an officer. Without further warning the soldiers open fire. They shoot straight into the crowd. Cries of fear and pain break out around you. Some people try to escape by climbing the walls around the meeting place. Many fall back, having been shot. Others search desperately for an exit. After six minutes the shooting stops. The soldiers march smartly out of the meeting place. Behind them lie at least 370 bodies and more than a thousand wounded.

These two pictures show the Amritsar massacre being carried out and Dyer's troops chasing demonstrators through Amritsar's streets. However, neither of them dates from the time of the events; both come from a film, Gandhi, made in the mid-1980s. Does this mean that they are unreliable as evidence of what actually happened? And is there any way in which a modern film can help our understanding of the past?

A plan of the Jallianwala Bagh. Find the evidence in the plan which shows that people in the Bagh could not have escaped Dyer's troops quickly and easily.

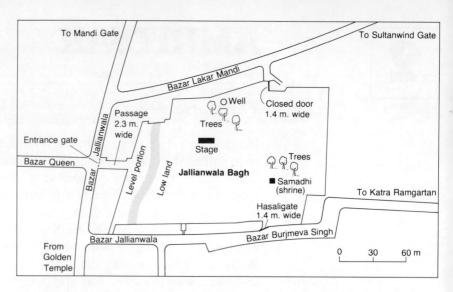

That is what happened on 13 April 1919, in the city of Amritsar in the Punjab. The soldiers were Indians of the British Indian Army. Their officers were British.

After the shooting, people living nearby rushed to the scene. Among them were Sardar Partap Singh, whose son had gone to the meeting. Later, he explained what he saw:

> *I did not enter the Bagh from the side which the soldiers had come out because I was afraid, but went round and entered by jumping over a wall. A dying man asked for water. When I tried to take water from a pit, I saw many dead bodies floating in it. Some living men had also hid themselves in it. I went to find my son. There were 800 or 1,000 wounded and dead lying near the walls besides others who ran away wounded and died either in their own houses or in the surrounding lanes. I could not find my son. I heard wailing of those shot and who were crying for water. Then I ran back home and heard my son was safe. I did not hear any proclamation forbidding people to attend public meetings.*
>
> Quoted in R. Furneaux's book, *Massacre at Amritsar*, 1963

Using the evidence: why did it happen?

13 April marked the start of a Sikh religious festival, when people poured into Amritsar, the site of the Sikhs' holy Golden Temple. Others came to the city to attend horse and cattle fairs. Some of the people in the Bagh that afternoon had come to listen to speeches attacking their British rulers, but many were more interested in having an enjoyable time, and had even brought blankets so they could make themselves comfortable. Yet the British authorities saw the gathering as a great threat. Why was this?

Search through the following statements and evidence from witnesses to see if you think the British were justified in acting as they did.

A In 1918–19 India was in a troubled condition. Many soldiers returning from the war could not find work; an influenza epidemic killed 12 million people; and Indian religious feelings were running high because of the part Britain played in the war, when she removed from power the Sultan of Turkey, the world's leading Muslim.

B The British tried to keep control by passing fierce laws allowing judges to hold trials and punish people without using juries. These 'Rowlatt laws' (named after the lawyer who drew them up) were most unpopular. Speakers in the Bagh on 13 April attacked them.

C The Punjab was in an especially restless state. Its Governor, Sir Michael O'Dwyer, believed in strict government. In Amritsar, crowds had attacked shops and banks, killed three British men and attacked three British women. One of the women was Marcia Sherwood, a doctor who worked among Indians. She was badly beaten and left for dead, but was saved by Hindus who found her and treated her.

D O'Dwyer called in the army to take charge in Amritsar. On 11 April General Dyer arrived with 474 British and 710 Indian soldiers. On the morning of 13 April Dyer's men toured the city for two hours reading out his order:

'No procession of any kind is permitted to parade in the streets. Any such procession, or gatherings of four men, will be treated as an unlawful assembly and dispersed by force of arms if necessary.'
       Quoted in R. Furneaux's book, *Massacre at Amritsar*, 1963

General Reginald Dyer. In 1919 he was 55 years old and had a sound record as a capable officer.

The gathering in the Bagh therefore broke this order. But the order had not been read out anywhere near the Bagh, even though Dyer knew that a meeting was planned there.

incensed: angry

E The leaders of Congress, an Indian political party which wanted Britain to give Indians far more power, declared:

The people of the Punjab were incensed against Sir Michael O'Dwyer by reason of his contempt and distrust of the educated classes, and by reason of the cruel and compulsory methods adopted during the war for obtaining recruits and money, and his suppression of public opinion by gagging the local press and shutting out nationalist newspapers from outside the Punjab.

The Rowlatt [laws] shook public confidence in the Government. . . . There was no conspiracy to overthrow the Government of the Punjab. . . . The arrest of three Indian leaders was the direct cause of the hysteria in Amritsar. . . .

The Jallianwala Bagh massacre was a calculated piece of inhumanity towards utterly innocent and unarmed men, including children, and unparalleled for its ferocity in the history of modern British administration.

The Congress Inquiry into Amritsar, 1919

F The British Government sent the Hunter Commission to investigate. The chief witness at its meetings was General Dyer. He explained first why he had felt that he had to act forcefully:

I was conscious of a great offensive movement gathering against me, and knew that to sit still would be fatal. When, therefore, the challenge by this movement in the shape of the assembly in the Jallianwala Bagh came to me, I knew that a military crisis had come, and that to view the assembly as a mere political gathering requiring simply to be asked to go away because it was there in breach of an order, was wholly remote from the facts and the necessities of the case. Amritsar was in fact the storm centre of a rebellion. The whole Punjab had its eyes on Amritsar, and the assembly of the crowd that afternoon was for all practical purposes a declaration of war by leaders whose hope and belief was that I should fail to take up the challenge.

General Dyer then answered questions from the Commission:

object: purpose

'In firing, was your object to disperse the crowd?'
'Yes.'
'Did the crowd at once start to disperse as soon as you fired?'
'Immediately.'
'Did you continue firing?'
'Yes.'
'If the crowd was going to disperse, why did you not stop firing?'
'I thought it my duty to go on firing until it dispersed. If I fired a little, the effect would not be sufficient.'
'What reason had you to suppose that if you had ordered the assembly to leave the Bagh, they would not have done so without the necessity of your firing?'

> *'Yes; I think it quite possible that I could have dispersed them even without firing.'*
> *'Why did you not adopt that course?'*
> *'I could not disperse them for some time; then they would all come back and laugh at me, and I considered I would be making myself a fool.'*
> *'In your view the situation was a very serious one?'*
> *'Very serious indeed, Sir.'*
>
> The Hunter Commission report, quoted in A. Draper's book, *The Amritsar Massacre*, 1981

G The official British paper, *The Civil and Military Gazette*, reported:

> *...an attempt to hold a proscribed meeting at Amritsar after the arrest of some ringleaders. The General, with only Indian troops and police, gave the orders to disperse. As the crowd refused to go, the order to fire was given. There were heavy casualties amongst the mob, several hundreds being killed and injured and there was no further trouble.*
>
> Quoted in A. Draper's book, as above

proscribed: banned

disperse: leave

1 Which of the above sources (**A–G**) are primary evidence?

2 a) List points in the sources that could be used to justify British action in Amritsar.
   b) List points that suggest General Dyer was wrong to act as he did.

3 a) Why did Dyer decide to do more than simply threaten the crowd?
   b) Do you think he was right?

4 Sources **E** and **F** both come from the time of the massacre.
   a) What are the main differences in these accounts of events in Amritsar?
   b) Why are they so different from each other?

5 a) How accurate a report does source **G** seem to be?
   b) What reasons can you think of to explain why this paper printed this sort of report?

Martial law

Dyer's superior, General Sir William Beynon, supported what Dyer had done. He sent a message: 'Your action correct and Lieutenant Governor [O'Dwyer] approves.' Dyer felt secure in proceeding with further harsh actions.

Martial law was declared in Amritsar, giving the army and police power to control affairs. Indians were ordered to bow every time they walked past a European. If they wished to go down the street where Marcia Sherwood was attacked, they had to wriggle or crawl along over the filth that covered its surface. Dyer explained:

meted: given

> *A helpless woman had been mercilessly beaten in a most cruel manner by a lot of cowards. She was beaten with sticks and shoes and knocked down six times. It seemed intolerable to me that some suitable punishment could not be meted out. Civil law is at an end and I search my brain for some punishment to meet the case.*
> Quoted in R. Furneaux's book, *Massacre at Amritsar*, 1963

Dyer also ordered a number of Indians to be punished by being whipped. Details of his actions soon reached Britain, and the Secretary of State for India, Edwin Montagu, became very alarmed. He said:

> *When you pass an order that all Indians must crawl past a particular place you are enforcing racial humiliation. When you put up a triangle where an outrage which we all deplore has taken place and whip people before they have been convicted, you are indulging in frightfulness. Are you going to keep your hold upon India by terrorism or are you going to rest it upon the growing goodwill of the people?*
> Quoted in A. Draper's book, *The Amritsar Massacre*, 1981

British soldiers enforcing Dyer's 'crawling' order on the street where a British doctor, Marcia Sherwood, had been savagely attacked.

Questions

1 In what ways do the views of Dyer and Montagu differ?

2 Why do these views differ so widely?

3 Whose view would you have supported? Give reasons for your answer.

4 Montagu used the word 'terrorism'. What do you believe this word means? Was he using it correctly?

The results of Amritsar

Did it prevent a rebellion in the Punjab?

The Hunter Commission spent weeks in India listening to witnesses. It decided:

> *The action taken by General Dyer has been described by others as having saved the situation in the Punjab and having averted a rebellion.... It does not appear to us possible to draw this conclusion. ...General Dyer acted beyond the necessity of the case, beyond what any reasonable man could have thought to be necessary.*
> Quoted in A. Draper's book, *The Amritsar Massacre*, 1981

But Miles Irving, a British official in the Punjab at the time, declared that as a result of Dyer's action:

> *The whole rebellion collapsed. Not only the mob that was fired upon dispersed and all trouble ceased in the city of Amritsar, but it was felt throughout the district. One of the reasons why there had been a danger was that the people not in the district thought for some reason or other that the Arm of Government was paralysed. The inaction of the police when the National Bank was burned lent some colour to that belief and there was an idea that the Government could do nothing, and this came as a disillusionment.*
>
> Quoted in General R.E.H. Dyer's pamphlet, *Army Disturbances in the Punjab*, HMSO, 1920

Did Dyer deserve to be punished?

One result of Amritsar was that it ended Dyer's career. He was made to resign and was called back to Britain.

Many people in Britain were horrified by Dyer's actions; others thought him a hero. *The Morning Post* called him 'The Man Who Saved India' and organised the raising of £26 000 for him. Edwin Montagu was attacked for dismissing Dyer; indeed, Montagu's eventual resignation was greeted in Parliament by loud cheering from the Tories.

An eminent Indian, Rabindranath Tagore, was in London at the time. He wrote home:

> *The result of the Dyer debates in both Houses of Parliament makes painfully evident the attitude of mind of the ruling classes of the country towards India. It shows that no outrage, however monstrous,*

The House of Lords debating the Dyer case on 20 July 1920. Many members stated that they supported Dyer and some strongly criticised Edwin Montagu. What sort of reasons might have caused the Lords to be so sympathetic to Dyer?

condonation: acceptance

> *committed against us by the agents of their Government, can arouse feelings of indignation in the hearts of those from whom our governors are chosen. The unashamed condonation of brutality expressed in their speeches and echoed in their newspapers is ugly in its frightfulness. The late events have conclusively proved that our true salvation lies in our own hands.*
>
> R. Tagore: *Letters to a Friend in India*, 1920

General Dyer lived in retirement until his death in 1927. Sir Michael O'Dwyer, the man who ruled the Punjab in 1919 and brought in Dyer's troops, was assassinated in London 13 years later, on 13 March 1940, by a Sikh from the Punjab who had come to Britain seeking vengeance for Amritsar.

Did Amritsar affect British rule in India?

The events of April 1919 came at a time when the liberal-minded Secretary of State for India, Edwin Montagu, was busy trying to increase the part Indians played in the government of their country. However, Amritsar did much to ruin Indian goodwill towards a policy of gradual change.

An Indian journalist, Frank Moraes, explained how Indians felt after Amritsar. He thought that far fewer Indians now believed that the British were wise rulers who deserved to be in charge.

> *We discussed it at school and felt horror and rage. Home late on holiday, I listened to my parents talking about it with their Indian friends. My father, a mild-tempered man, was almost speechless with indignation on reading in a newspaper of the presentation of a gold sword to General Dyer by 'the Ladies of England'. In his autobiography Nehru describes how, some months after the Jallianwala Bagh tragedy, he travelled by the night train from Amritsar to Delhi, and was kept awake by a red-faced British general talking to a British colleague. The General, clad 'in pyjamas with bright pink stripes', declaimed at the top of his voice on how he had dealt with a crowd of natives in Amritsar. It was Dyer.*
>
> *Imperialism, when it cannot rule by compromises, can only impose its authority by force. If in Gandhi's later campaigns of civil disobedience the Raj did not use force, it is not because it developed a sudden tenderness for Indian nationalism but because the backlash of Jallianwala Bagh deterred it: another massacre would have meant a countrywide uprising and the use of perpetual force to hold India down.*
>
> F. Moraes: *Witness to an Era*, 1973

Instead of winning the cooperation of most educated Indians, Montagu's reforms were attacked. Indians began to protest more often, on a bigger scale, and with more success. At the forefront of these protests was the Congress Party.

Questions

1. Miles Irving's views on the results of Amritsar are very different from those of the Hunter Commission.
   a) Describe the main differences between them.
   b) Why do you think they are so different?

2. Which source or sources in the section above suggest that Amritsar was going to result in more forceful Indian opposition to the Raj? Quote the passages that support your choice of evidence.

3. How might either a British or an Indian newspaper have reported O'Dwyer's death? Write the report from either point of view, in about 150 words.

THE INDIA ACT, 1919

The Viceroy

— Advised by a Council of six civilians (three of them Indian) and the Commander in Chief of the British Army in India. Could enforce laws even when the Central Legislature refused to pass them. Chose his own officials.

The Central Legislature

The Council of State
— 17 000 very rich people could vote for it.
The Central Assembly
— nearly a million wealthy people could vote for it.

Both had a minority of members chosen by the Viceroy, as well as elected majorities.

Provincial governments

In provinces other than the princely states, power was divided between British officials and ministers chosen by elected Indian assemblies. Fifteen million better-off Indians (including women) could vote. This divided system of power was called 'dyarchy'.

Controlled by the British:	Controlled by Indian ministers:
Finance	Education
Police	Agriculture
Justice	Health
	Public works

Question

Why do you think the Raj kept control of finance, the police and justice?

3 GANDHI AND THE CONGRESS PARTY

If you had been an ordinary Indian angered by the Rowlatt laws and by Amritsar, what might you have done? It is very likely that you would have looked for an anti-British organisation to join. In 1919 the most important of these was the Congress Party.

The early years of the Congress Party

In a country of vast size and many languages it was not easy to set up a national political party. It was the British who helped to make this possible. Railways, the telegraph and postal services all assisted the organising of a national body. The schools, colleges and universities set up by the British turned out people who could speak the same language – English. Educated Indians who found it almost impossible to enter the ICS naturally felt resentful at being shut out of the government of their own country. In 1885 a number of discontented Indians, chiefly drawn from the educated minority, gathered together to form the Congress Party. They asked for a share in ruling India.

Two different views are given below as to whether Congress was right to press for a share in government. The first comes from Annie Besant, a remarkable English woman who went to India and helped found the Congress Party. At the party's first meeting, she heard the President of Congress say:

'Indians are British citizens and claim all British citizens' rights. The first of these is freedom.' He then claimed for Indians in India all the control that Englishmen had in England. This was a necessity, in order to remedy the great economic evil which was at the root of Indian poverty. It was 'absolutely necessary' for the progress and welfare of the Indian people. 'The whole matter can be comprised in one word, Self-Government, or Swaraj.' When should a beginning be made which should automatically develop into full Self-Government? At once. 'Not only has the time fully arrived, but had arrived long past.'
Annie Besant: *How India Wrought for Freedom*, 1915

The Viceroy in 1885 was Lord Dufferin. He felt that the time had not come for spreading democracy in India. He wrote:

The people of India are not the 7000 students at universities, but the millions whom neither education nor the influence of European ideas have transformed. We are under the shadow of an enormous danger

— the overpopulation of the country. Where is there a more crying need for sanitary reform than amongst those who insist on bathing in their tanks of drinking water and where millions die of disease? What misery is spread amongst millions of women by the immoral custom of child marriage! Yet where have any of these been the subject of serious enquiry [by Congress]? The fact is that Congress is the product of a tiny section of the Indian community touched by European education, ideas and literature. They neither represent the aristocratic section of Indian society, nor are they in contact with the great mass of the population: they do not understand their wants or necessities.

Quoted in C.H. Philips' book, *The Evolution of India and Pakistan*, 1962

Questions

1. a) What reasons for Indian self-government are offered in the extract from Annie Besant's book?
   b) What reasons are offered by Lord Dufferin to support his view that self-government was quite inappropriate?

2. Which argument do you find the more convincing? Give reasons for your answer.

The British Government eventually reformed Indian government in 1909. The Indian Councils Act was the joint work of John Morley, the Liberal Secretary of State for India, and Lord Minto, the Viceroy. The reform allowed Indians to be appointed to the Council that advised the Viceroy, and elected to the councils that advised the governors of the provinces, but they had no real power. The continued complaints of Indians, and a growing feeling among some British politicians that India ought to move towards self-government, led to Edwin Montagu's 1919 reform establishing dyarchy. Throughout these years Congress remained a small party mainly supported by wealthy Indians. Its early leaders were men like G.K. Gokhale, who thought Indians should respect British rule and proceed very slowly and lawfully towards their aim of self-government; only a minority, led by B.G. Tilak, were ready to use force. But in 1919 this mood was shattered.

Gandhi

Within a few years, Congress changed from being a party for the privileged few into a party for the mass of Indian people. The key figure in this change was Mohandas Karamchand Gandhi. He was born in 1869 into a well-to-do family, his father being an important administrator in various princely states. Gandhi studied law in Britain, and between 1893 and 1914 practised law in South Africa. Here he suffered insults because of his colour and fought for the rights of Indian people living in South Africa. He developed a method of non-violent protest, such as leading a peaceful march of Indians to places where they were not supposed to go. During World War I he returned to India and supported the British war effort. By this time his deep religious feelings had come to dominate his life. He lived very simply in an ashram, a place of religious study. The Rowlatt laws and Amritsar transformed Gandhi's attitude; he became convinced that the British should leave India. He joined the Congress Party and remained the most important person in it for most of his life. Such was the quality of his life that he was often called the 'Mahatma', meaning the 'Great Soul'.

Using the evidence: what was Gandhi like?

A
M.K. Gandhi, 1869–1948. In about 1915 Gandhi gave up wearing Western-style clothes; instead he dressed in a simple home-spun 'dhoti' (loin cloth). He began spinning thread to show that he believed in the importance of humble work and to encourage Indians to use home-made cloth.

The following statements were all made by people who knew Gandhi.

B Jawaharlal Nehru was a member of the Congress Party who, at an early age, worked closely with Gandhi.

He made rather astounding proposals asking, for instance, lawyers to give up their practice, and live simply and on next to nothing; everybody [was] to wear handspun clothes made in the villages; and the whole atmosphere changed, and many of our older leaders were not quite clear what all this meant, because they'd been thinking differently. But he caught on so well with the Indian people, the masses, that older leaders were pulled then towards him. The fact that stood out about Gandhi was how he attracted people of different kinds and thereby he became a link between different groups from the poorest peasant, whom he always sought to represent, to princes and rich industrialists. He was certainly the biggest individual that I have come across in my life.

Quoted in F.H. Watson and H. Tennyson's book, *Talking of Gandhi*, 1969

C   Here is the view of an Indian journalist:

emaciated: very thin

Gandhi, with his emaciated shrunken figure and his gnome-like face behind metal-rimmed glasses, was not impressive at first sight. He had, however, a magnificent head, and his bare chest was nobly proportioned, his voice low, and his manner in an odd but striking way was somehow kingly. Gandhi was often mild but he was never really meek. His eyes, as I noticed later, could sometimes be stony.

F. Moraes: *Witness to an Era*, 1973

D   Arvind Nehra was an Indian, educated in Cambridge, who rose to be a judge under the Raj. In the 1920s he wrote of Gandhi:

His ideals are about as unattainable as those with which I left Cambridge. I, also, was going to make a new heaven and a new earth, and bring about a better understanding between black men and white men, and it all seemed so very easy. . . .

khaddar: cotton cloth produced in India

Gandhi, I see, preaches that everyone must do without foreign goods and wear only the native manufactured 'khaddar'. So for interest's sake I sat down and worked this out the other night, only to discover there would be something like three inches of khaddar per head of the population, and since even the loin cloth of my people requires more than this, lo, another distant Utopia!

A. Nehra: *Letters to an English Gentlewoman*, 1978

1   Using all the above sources, write a short account describing Gandhi to someone who has no knowledge of him. Mention his appearance and his beliefs.

2   Do any of the sources suggest that Gandhi's approach was successful? If so, quote words and phrases from the sources in your answer.

3   a) Which source criticises Gandhi?
    b) Why might the writer be likely to criticise Gandhi?

Gandhi in action

How could a man who opposed violence make the British leave India? Gandhi explained his method of opposition. He hoped to win over the British by showing them that his cause was noble and just. He wrote:

> *I seek to blunt the edge of the tyrant's sword, not by putting up against it a sharper-edged weapon, but by disappointing his expectation that I should be offering physical resistance. The resistance of the soul that I should offer instead would at first dazzle him, and at last compel recognition from him, which recognition would not humiliate him but would uplift him.*
>
> Quoted in B.N. Pandey's book, *The Break-up of British India*, 1969

In 1919 and 1920 Gandhi organised different sorts of protests. For example, he called for a 'hartal', a day when all business stopped. He also criticised the heavy taxes that the British imposed on the ordinary peasants (the 'ryots'), which left them with little money to buy tools and fertilisers and often forced them into debt. In 1921 he urged Indians not to pay the tax. He also called for large peaceful gatherings to protest against British rule. By 1930 he had found a new target – the salt tax. The production of salt was a government monopoly and a heavy tax was placed on it, so Gandhi led around 80 followers on a 24-day march to the coast, with the declared intention of making salt from sea water. One of his fellow marchers recalled how, when they arrived, Gandhi went down to the water's edge:

> *...on the sand there are some deposits of salt left when the water has receded. So he just picked it up, a pinch of salt, and gave it to the next person who was standing by – I don't recollect his or her name – and that was a symbol of breaking the Salt Act. Some photographers took pictures, and then later on there was a prayer, and then he went back to his work.*
>
> Quoted in F.H. Watson and H. Tennyson's book, *Talking of Gandhi*, 1969

On 6 April 1930 Gandhi deliberately broke the law by making salt and called on the whole of India to defy this law. The picture shows some of his followers evaporating sea water to make salt. Gandhi was arrested when he went on to invade a salt works.

Gandhi's efforts won enormous publicity, and his simple life and religious devotion attracted many Indians. Women, especially, began to feel that they had a powerful part to play. As one of them, Aruna Asaf Ali, put it:

> *A woman was made to feel the equal of man. The real liberation of Indian women can be traced to this period, the 1930s. No single act could have done what Gandhi did when he first called upon women to join and said 'They are the better symbols of mankind'.*
> Quoted in Z. Masani's book, *Indian Tales of the Raj*, 1987

Gandhi wanted to unite all Indians, and he tried hard to draw into his campaigns the lowest caste in Hindu society, the untouchables. He called them 'Harijans', which meant 'children of God'. They were led by a very distinguished lawyer and educator, Dr B.R.

The struggle against the British led to outbreaks of violence.
Right: Gandhi's supporters being arrested by police who are carrying 'laths' (long sticks) which they used to beat demonstrators.
Below right: this is an officially approved photograph showing the bodies of 21 policemen killed in Chauri Chaura by a rioting mob. The police station was set on fire and the policemen thrown in the flames.
Below: this photograph was taken in 1927 in Amritsar. It shows troops with bayonets fixed to their rifles confronting a crowd of demonstrators.

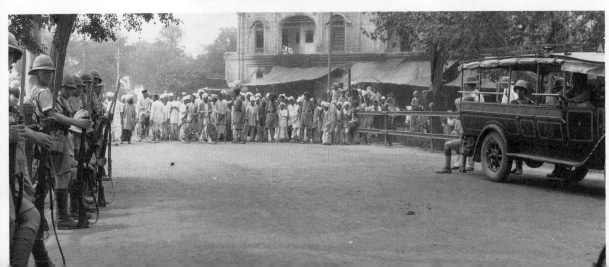

Ambedkar. Ambedkar saw Gandhi as a higher-caste leader and never trusted him. Gandhi also sought to persuade Muslims that Congress was not just for Hindus; indeed, after 1931 he spent much of his time trying to get the different communities in India to cooperate, but he was not as successful in this as he would have wished. He was also deeply concerned about the poverty of Indian farmers. His campaign to persuade Indians to wear khaddar was both an attack on the British textile industry and an attempt to improve the lives of country folk by giving them more work. He encouraged the setting up of simple, small-scale industries in the villages. Some Congress members thought his ideas were out of date.

From time to time Gandhi was imprisoned, and from time to time he went on a fast to draw attention to something that he thought was wrong, such as the killings at Chauri Chaura in 1922 or the fighting between Muslims and Hindus in the North-West Frontier Provinces in 1924. Gandhi declared he had no personal hatred for the British and indeed made friends with many of them. Lord Irwin, who was Viceroy from 1926 to 1931, was a deeply religious man. He held many serious discussions with Gandhi during 1930.

According to M.R. Masani, a Congress Party official:

If the Nazis had been there they would have executed Gandhi long before he became effective; but the British played ball with him. Gandhi was shrewd enough to utilize the nature of British rule in India to win independence without too much bloodshed.

Quoted in Z. Masani's book, *Indian Tales of the Raj*, 1987

Questions

1 Briefly list the ways in which Gandhi opposed the British Government.

2 Why do you think he used these methods instead of more violent ones?

3 Why were women especially ready to follow Gandhi?

4 What evidence shows that Gandhi wanted a consensus, a harmony, of all Indian society?

5 Why do you think one individual could achieve so much?

Other Congress leaders

Although Gandhi was the most important member of Congress, he was not the only leading figure. According to Aruna Asaf Ali:

All the leadership had spent their early years in England. They were influenced by British thought, British ideas, that is why our leaders

were always telling the British 'How can you do these things? They're against your own basic values'. We had no hatred, in fact it was the other way round — it was their values that made us revolt.
Quoted in Z. Masani's book, *Indian Tales of the Raj*, 1987

One of these leaders was Jawaharlal Nehru. The Nehrus were a wealthy Kashmiri family, members of the highest caste, the Brahmins. Nehru's father was a lawyer who followed a very British lifestyle. Nehru went to Harrow School and Cambridge University before becoming a lawyer. However, Amritsar upset him deeply and Gandhi impressed him greatly, although he did not share Gandhi's rural-religious vision of India. In 1936 he declared:

The only key to the solution of India's problems lies in socialism. I see no way of ending the poverty, the vast unemployment of the Indian people, except through socialism. That involves vast changes in our political and social structure, the ending of vested interests in land and industry, as well as the princely Indian States system....
Some glimpse we can have of this new civilization in the territories of the USSR. Much has happened there with which I disagree, but I look upon that great unfolding of a new civilization as the most promising feature of our dismal age.

ideology: beliefs

How does socialism fit in with the present ideology of the Congress? I do not think it does. I believe in the rapid industrialization of the country and only thus I think will the standards of the people rise substantially and poverty be combated.
Quoted in C.H. Philips' book, *The Evolution of India and Pakistan*, 1962

Like Gandhi, Nehru took part in peaceful protests and served prison sentences for his activities. But there were others who were less convinced that protest should always be peaceful. In particular the left-winger Subhas Chandra Bose, President of Congress 1938–9, had different views. According to someone who knew him:

Jawaharlal was essentially a kind of Englishman. Bose was a Bengali and he would die for India. When he was in college the Principal, an Englishman, said something to him about India. He caught hold of the Principal by the scruff of the neck, dragged him down a staircase and threw him down. That was his temperament — he came to boiling point when it came to India.
Quoted in Z. Masani's book, *Indian Tales of the Raj*, 1987

Nor were all protests peaceful. In 1930, for example, the city of Peshawar slipped for a time from British control when Indian troops refused to deal with anti-British demonstrations. A report sent to the British Government in that year listed the following events:

18th April. Chittagong raid, railway officer shot dead, set fire to buildings. Several wounded and policeman murdered.

22nd April. Senior Police Inspector shot dead at Geni.
25th August. Bomb thrown at Calcutta Police Commissioner.
29th August. Inspector General of Police died of wounds.
30th August. Bombs thrown into homes of police inspector and excise sub-inspector in Mymensingh.
8th December. Inspector General of Prisons, Bengal, shot dead in his office.

Quoted in W. Golant's book, *The Long Afternoon*, 1975

Questions

1 In what ways did the behaviour of the Congress Party change between 1885 and 1930?

2 Why did Congress change during this period?

3 Briefly explain how Nehru's view of India's future differed from Gandhi's.

4 Why did Aruna Asaf Ali think that British and Indian nationalists should be able to live in harmony, not conflict?

Further attempts at reform

By 1930 the Congress Party was demanding complete independence from British rule. The British were not prepared to agree to this, but both the Labour and Conservative leaders, Ramsay MacDonald and Stanley Baldwin, who between them led Britain from 1924 to 1937, came to think that India must be allowed to move gradually towards becoming a dominion, a country in the Empire that managed its own affairs. In 1929 the Viceroy, Lord Irwin, announced:

It is the desire of the British Government that India should, in the fullness of time, take her place in the Empire in equal partnership with the Dominions.

Quoted in B.N. Pandey's book, *The Indian Nationalist Movement*, 1974

Some British politicians followed Winston Churchill in opposing this idea, but they were in the minority. It was not easy, however, to follow a policy of slow change when Congress was demanding that it should be swift. In 1930, after the Simon Commission (1928) had failed to come up with an answer, the Labour Government decided to try to get together all the important leaders of Indian opinion at 'round table' conferences. Congress refused to send anyone to the first meeting. In 1931 it changed its mind and sent Gandhi, who had to be released from jail to attend the conference. Frank Moraes did not think that he made a good delegate:

Right: *a crowd of demonstrators showing what they think of Sir John Simon's visit to India in 1928. He came to try to work out a plan for ending trouble in India. All Indian groups turned down his schemes and complained that his seven-man commission did not include any Indians.*

Below: *a meeting of the Round Table Conference, 1931, in St James's Palace, London. Note the contrast between Gandhi's dress and that of the other delegates.*

the depressed classes: the untouchables
repudiated: rejected

Gandhi made the fatal error of claiming to speak for the Muslims and the depressed classes, the spokesmen of both communities repudiated him, and since the Muslims then numbered nearly thirty per cent of the population and the depressed classes about twenty per cent it was difficult for him to sustain his claim that he represented ninety-five per cent of India. The minorities, comprising of Muslims, depressed classes, a section of Indian Christians, the Anglo-Indians and the British community, then confronted the British Government with an agreement arrived at between themselves. Whitehall had no alternative but to announce that the government would make its own decision.

F. Moraes: *Witness to an Era*, 1973

A cartoon that appeared in Punch in January 1931. It was published at a time when British politicians were discussing giving more power to Indians. Do you think the cartoonist agreed with this policy?

A QUESTION OF CONTROL.

INDIA. "WHAT ABOUT CHANGING PLACES?"
JOHN BULL. "WELL, YOU'RE WELCOME TO SEE WHAT YOU CAN DO AT THE WHEEL; BUT I THINK I'D BETTER SIT BESIDE YOU—WITHIN REACH OF THE BRAKE."

The British Government pushed ahead with a new reform which finally became the 1935 Government of India Act. Although Nehru was against cooperation, Congress agreed to take part in elections for provincial governments in 1937. It won more than 700 of the 1585 seats and formed governments in seven provinces. According to Frank Moraes:

On the whole, the record of the Congress provincial ministries in their two years in office was creditable. Whether they liked it or not, Congressmen were beginning to think constitutionally. Their relations with the governors were almost uniformly cordial. Congress leaders gained valuable administrative experience which stood them in good stead later.

F. Moraes: *Witness to an Era*, 1973

cordial: friendly

impending: coming

In 1936 the Governor of one Indian province, the United Provinces, commented on the results of the 1935 Act:

The sense of impending change awakened the villages. The Government, which had opposed the Congress with the weight of its authority, now stood inactive. The villager felt that the British Raj was weakening, that the Congress Raj was coming, and, as so often happens, threw himself definitely on what seemed to be the winning side.

Quoted in H.V. Hodson's book, *The Great Divide*, 1969

Congress had come a long way since 1918, yet the Indian people were far from united behind it. It faced a struggle, not only with the Raj, but with a rival group – the Muslim League.

THE INDIA ACT, 1935

(Burma was separated off from India and given its own government.)

Central Government

i) The Viceroy kept control of law and order and finance and could reject laws passed by the Assembly.
ii) The Council of State, chosen from the provinces of British India and (40 per cent of total) the princely states.
iii) The Legislative Assembly, two-thirds elected by the richest 14 per cent of the population, one-third chosen by the rulers of princely states.

(In fact the princes refused to cooperate. This part of the Act never worked properly.)

Provincial Government (excluding princely states)

Assemblies chose ministers who had proper control of government; the 1919 dyarchy system of sharing power was abolished. Thirty million Indians could vote, i.e., about a sixth of all adult Indians.

Question

Imagine that it is 1935 and you are a writer working on a British or Indian newspaper. You have to explain the 1935 Act to your readers.
a) Explain why you think the British decided to pass the Act.
b) Describe the main changes that the Act will make.
c) Discuss whether or not you believe that the Act deserves to be praised and supported.

4 JINNAH AND THE MUSLIM LEAGUE

In the early twentieth century an Englishman called Radclyffe Sidebottom worked as a Calcutta river pilot. His main fear was not that Indians might attack him, but that he might be caught up in terrible events in which Indians attacked each other. He described what these events were like:

> *The high-pitched screaming of the rioting crowd was something that you could never forget. You'd hear the screaming coming towards you, they would commit some horrible act and then patter away without a sound. But it wasn't so much the sounds, it was the smell of fear — and you'd get the smell of fear not necessarily from those who were being killed, but from the rioting mobs that were doing the killing. The moment the crowd decided that one of the opposite religion had been killed, then everybody in one form of dress would turn on the others and in a matter of forty-eight hours there were three hundred, four hundred deaths a night. If you saw a man writhing in agony and you stopped your car and got out to help him — then you were finished.*
> Quoted in C. Allen's book, *Plain Tales from the Raj*, 1975

Large numbers of followers of two quite different religions — Hindus and Muslims — lived in Calcutta. They attacked each other in many other towns and villages, too. In 1922 rioting by a Muslim group of mixed Indian–Arab origin, called the Moplahs, led to the death of 600 Hindus. Between 1923 and 1928 government figures showed that there had been 112 serious clashes which had left 450 dead and 5000 seriously injured. Why should Indians, eager to see the British leave their land, turn to fighting one another?

Important religions in India

Hinduism
There have been Hindus in India for 2000 years. Hindus see the whole of creation as divine. They can worship many different gods who each represent a different part of 'the divine'. They study several different religious books, not just one. Hindus believe each creature has a soul that is a tiny part of 'Brahman', the great world soul. The soul can be reborn many times; the body it is born into depends on the kind of life that has just been lived. Hindu society is full of rules that must be followed. These include the division of society into four major castes: priests; leaders and warriors; merchants

and businessmen; and peasants. Below them are the 'untouchables', who are outside the castes. A Hindu cannot marry into another caste, or move from one caste to another except through the reward or punishment at the end of life that leads to rebirth into a different caste. Hindus are fond of depicting their gods in statues and pictures.

Islam

Islam was inspired by Muhammad, who was born in the year 570. He is seen by the followers of Islam (Muslims) as their Great Prophet. Through him the one god in whom Muslims believe set down his holy words in a book called the Koran. Muslims dislike trying to depict God in pictures and statues. They first invaded India in the thirteenth century. In 1526 their leader, Babur, set himself up as Mogul Emperor in India. The Moguls ruled much of India until the British arrived and eventually destroyed their power.

Sikhs

The Sikh faith emerged in one part of India, the Punjab. It was developed over 200 years by ten wise leaders or 'gurus', starting in the fifteenth century. The gurus were Hindus who tried to develop a new faith that took account of Muslim beliefs. Like Muslims, they followed one god. They were persecuted and became very fine warriors in order to fight for survival.

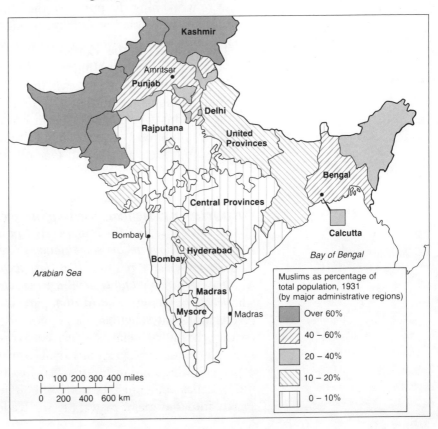

This map shows the parts of India where most Muslims lived. What difficulties does it suggest faced anyone trying to create a separate country for Muslim Indians?

The Muslims of India

The Muslims never managed to conquer the whole of India, but over the centuries they did gain control of the north of the country. They managed to convert some Hindus – especially untouchables – to their belief in one god and his prophet Muhammad. Muslims usually disliked the Hindu faith. In the early twentieth century one of them noted:

> *We were so far apart that, although we lived next door to each other, we didn't intermarry, we didn't eat together, we were not called to each other's ceremonies. So we became quite distinct.*
> Quoted in B. Lapping's book, *End of Empire*, 1985

By the early twentieth century many Muslim leaders were becoming worried about the future of their faith. Their worries were caused by the following factors:

a) The success of a Hindu group called Arya Samaj. It aimed to convert Muslims to the Hindu faith. Between 1907 and 1910 more than a thousand Muslims changed their beliefs.

b) The setting up in 1915 of Hindu Mahasabha. This group worked to make Hindus far more powerful and independent. They were quite prepared to use force against people whom they thought were weakening the purity of the Hindu faith. It was one of their number who was, eventually, to murder Gandhi.

c) The growth of the Congress Party. Congress tried to recruit Muslims, as well as Hindus, and a number of Muslims did join. However, it remained overwhelmingly a party made up of Hindus. Some Muslims feared that if India ever became a free democracy, the Hindus would always be in power since they were so much more numerous. Even when Congress was first set up, some Muslim leaders attacked it. One of them, Sir Sayid Ahmad Khan, complained of Congress:

> *They do not take into consideration that India is inhabited by different nationalities; they suppose that the Muslims, the Sikhs, the Bengalis, and the Peshawaris can all be treated alike and all of them belong to the same nation. The Congress thinks that they follow the same religion, that they speak the same language, that their way of life and customs are the same and that their attitude to history is similar. The Muslims are in a minority but they are a highly united minority.*
> Quoted in M. Yapp's book, *The British Raj and Indian Nationalism*, 1977

Lord Minto, Viceroy of India in the early twentieth century.

Question

As a British official, prepare a report for the Viceroy called 'The Hindu-Muslim problem'. In your report explain the reasons for the problem; describe events that you feel should worry the Raj; and say what you think should be done about the problem.

The Muslim response

If you had been a Muslim living in India in the early part of this century, what actions might you have welcomed to protect the followers of your religion? Some leaders thought that the right answer was to win a special political position from the British. In 1875 Sayid Ahmad Khan had set up Aligarh College; here Muslims could learn the English language and become better equipped to deal with the Raj. In 1906 a number of Muslim leaders gathered in Dacca and formed an organisation called the All-India Muslim League. Their aim was to persuade the British to support their demands for a special political position in India. The Viceroy of the time was Lord Minto. He was ready to listen to them.

Minto was being pressed by John Morley, the Secretary of State for India, to reform the Raj, but he was not very enthusiastic about giving in to the Congress Party's demands for more power. He decided that allowing Muslims special rights would divide his Indian opponents and encourage Muslims to look to Britain for support. The 1909 Indian Councils Act guaranteed Muslims their own representatives on the councils set up in all the provinces. These representatives were chosen by Muslims voting quite separately from anyone else. Muslims were also sure of having at least six places on the Viceroy's council.

At this time the League was not a large-scale popular organisation. Most of its members were wealthy people. Events in the following years, however, were to greatly alter this situation. Feelings between Hindus and Muslims became so bitter that out of the struggle for freedom from British rule came not one united India, but two quite separate countries.

Events in the outside world encouraged Muslims to think about the importance of defending their faith. During 1912 and 1913 Turkey was defeated by the Balkan countries. Muslims regarded the Sultan of Turkey as their Caliph, their most important spiritual leader, yet the British seemed to be hostile to him. When World War I began, Turkey joined forces with Germany; Turkish and British troops therefore fought against one another. Once the war was over, Britain helped to draw up the Treaty of Sèvres, which greatly reduced the size of Turkey and removed the Sultan from power. In India, an organisation known as the Khilafat was set up in 1919 to support the Caliph. Its founders were two former students of Aligarh College: Shaukat and Muhammad Ali. The Khilafat not only spread the message that it was important to fight for Muslim beliefs, but also stirred up anti-British feelings in the villages. The riot by the Moplahs in 1922 was caused by the way the police behaved when chasing Khilafat leaders. The movement faded once its leaders had been imprisoned and the Turks had settled down to accept that their Sultan had gone forever and that Turkey was now a republic. But in India the Khilafat's legacy was a far greater tension between Hindus and Muslims, as well as between Muslims and the British.

Questions

1 Why did the British Raj give the Muslims special guarantees in 1909?

2 Do you think this was a wise policy to follow? Give reasons for your answer.

3 List the main events that led to anti-British feeling among many Muslims after World War I.

Jinnah

During the 1920s Gandhi was busy turning Congress into a party with mass support. But the Muslim League did not grow in the same sort of way; indeed, the League faced rivals for Muslim support such as the All-India Muslim Conference. Nor did the League have a popular and important leader. The man who was to become the League's great leader was, at first, a keen supporter of Congress. Frank Moraes knew Muhammad Ali Jinnah well and described him as:

> *...tall, thin and elegant, with a monocle on a grey silk cord and a stiff white collar which he wore in the hottest weather. Jinnah was one of the very few intellectually honest politicians I have known. Humility was not one of his strong points, but there was no humbug in his makeup. Like every decent-minded thoughtful Indian he wanted his country to be politically free. The British completely misread the character and aims of this dedicated man. They had been accustomed to deal with a type of Muslim leader whose dislike for the Congress could be encouraged by official favours. But Jinnah had no purchase price.*
>
> F. Moraes: *Witness to an Era*, 1973

M.A. Jinnah, 1876–1948. The son of a merchant, he went to a Christian missionary school, and then to Britain to study law. Jinnah was one of a number of Muslims who joined the Congress Party.

Questions

1 What evidence in the above extract shows that Frank Moraes supported Indian independence?

2 What do you think the last sentence in this extract means?

At first, Jinnah's aim was for Congress and the League to work together. However, although he joined the Congress Party in 1906, he did not attend a League conference until 1912. By then he was becoming an important figure and served for a while as a member of the Viceroy's Council, elected by Bombay's Muslims. In 1914 he arranged for the League and Congress conferences to be held in Bombay at the same time so that they could cooperate. In 1916 he was one of the leaders who signed the Lucknow Pact, in which both organisations demanded a proper national assembly elected by Indians voting in separate communities. This would allow Muslims to choose their own delegates. The Pact also promised Muslims a guaranteed number of assembly seats in provinces where Muslims were in a minority. Jinnah seemed to be one of the most enthusiastic Muslim leaders, eager to show that Congress was not just a Hindu organisation. Yet in a few years' time he was to become the Congress Party's most bitter opponent. Why did this happen?

The growth of the idea of Pakistan

Jinnah disagreed with Gandhi's methods of protest using large numbers of people. He therefore left the Congress Party in 1920 and showed his readiness to work with the British by rejoining the Viceroy's Council in 1923. For the next few years he concentrated on persuading the British to protect the Muslims. In 1928 Nehru produced plans for the government of a free India that greatly alarmed Jinnah. Nehru would not agree to Jinnah's demand that Muslims would be guaranteed a third of the seats in a future parliament. Jinnah left India in despair and went to live in Britain.

In 1935 Jinnah returned to India, and two years later the League took part in the elections for the new provincial assemblies. The League did badly, winning only 108 seats. Even in provinces where Muslims were in the majority it was not League representatives but other Muslims who were usually elected. Frank Moraes saw how Jinnah's remaining hopes were dashed:

Jinnah with the Labour politician Stafford Cripps. Cripps tried several times to find a peaceful solution to the problem of how to increase the Indians' share in the government of their country.

> *Jinnah was confident of forming some coalition ministries with Congress. Congress, flushed with victory, would have none of it and would take in Muslim representatives only on condition they became members of Congress.*
>
> *Jinnah was furious. In the minds of Jinnah and the League, Congress rule now came to mean Hindu domination. Until then Jinnah had never thought in terms of mass contacts. Now he realised that without the support of the Muslim masses the League could not pose an effective challenge to Congress.*
>
> F. Moraes: *Witness to an Era*, 1973

Nehru felt that it was safe to ignore Jinnah. In the United Provinces, for example, the League had won only 27 out of 228 seats. Its demand for a third of all government posts seemed absurd. Gandhi tried in vain to persuade Jinnah to work with Congress. Jinnah was determined to make the League into a mass movement that would fight for Muslim rights. He often made statements like these:

> *Congress leaders may shout as much as they like that Congress is a national body. But I say it is not true. Congress is nothing but a Hindu body. The presence of a few Muslims, a few misled and misguided ones, does not make it a national body. The Congress, no doubt, is the largest single party. But it is nothing more than that.*
>
> Quoted in B.N. Pandey's book, *The Indian Nationalist Movement*, 1974

The League spread to many towns and villages; its low subscriptions encouraged ordinary Muslims to join. As President, Jinnah toured the country making speeches, building up the organisation, and stressing to Muslims that their faith was in danger. By March 1940 he had persuaded his followers to agree to the 'Lahore Resolution':

A Muslim demonstration in Calcutta, where about a quarter of the population were followers of Islam.

It is the considered view of this session of the All-India Muslim League that no constitutional plan would be workable in this country or acceptable to the Muslims unless it is designed on the following principle — the areas in which the Muslims are in a majority, as in the north-western and eastern zones of India, should be grouped to constitute 'independent states': adequate safeguards should be provided for minorities.

Quoted in C.H. Philips' book, *The Evolution of India and Pakistan*, 1962

British leaders had promised that India would become a dominion. It now seemed as if the main threat to peaceful progress towards this goal was division between the Indians themselves.

Questions

1 Under the heading 'Why Jinnah changed his mind', write a short explanation of why Jinnah switched from being a member of Congress to being its opponent.

2 How might a journalist on a Congress newspaper have reported the Lahore Resolution to its readers?

3 Do you think that the British were pleased about these developments? Give reasons for your answer.

5 CRISIS, 1939-46

War

In 1942 K.F. Rustamji, a young Indian, was serving as a police officer in his own country. He had to deal with many serious outbreaks of violence in a very difficult situation. He explained:

inciting: stirring up

> While I was dealing with the riots, my brother was inciting them. He was a professor and behind a large amount of student agitation. All the time my family was telling me to get out of the police force. There was a conflict in my mind, as there must have been in the mind of every Indian at that time, whether to support the British or throw them out.
>
> Quoted in Z. Masani's book, *Indian Tales of the Raj*, 1987

The problem facing this young Indian was caused by the outbreak of World War II in September 1939. This event upset the fairly peaceful progress the Raj was enjoying after the introduction of the 1935 India Act, and brought back conflict between Indian nationalists and their British rulers. Congress leaders were angry at the way the Viceroy, Lord Linlithgow, declared that India was at war with Germany without consulting them, so they resigned from all their posts in provincial governments. As the war began to go increasingly badly for Britain, so Congress was torn between not wanting to see Britain defeated by Fascists, yet wanting to use this chance to win the campaign for freedom.

An army recruit receiving money for joining the Indian Army. The army grew from around 200 000 to well over two million in strength. This huge increase came not from conscripts but from volunteers.

In 1940 Britain seemed in danger of invasion by Germany. In December 1941 Japan entered the war. In February 1942 Japanese forces took Singapore, invaded Burma and by March had reached the frontiers of India. Meanwhile, Japanese warships sank British ships in the Indian Ocean. In this crisis Britain's efforts to win Indian support seemed to the Indians to be feeble. Linlithgow promised that India would become a dominion some time after the war, and that he would add Indians to his wartime councils. Also in 1942, the Labour politician Stafford Cripps made firm offers of dominion status and promised that Indians could choose an assembly at the end of the war to plan their own government. However, he could not offer the Indians any immediate power, and was unable to give them control over the armed forces and defence. He also alarmed Congress by saying that provinces which did not wish to join a free postwar India could become separate dominions. Congress leaders felt that Britain was losing the war, and in June 1942 they demanded that Britain should end the Raj at once. When Britain refused, Congress started a 'Quit India' campaign, to drive out the British. It was this trouble that K.F. Rustamji struggled to control.

Questions

1 K.F. Rustamji's family tried to persuade him to leave the police force.
   a) What sort of arguments might they have used?
   b) How might he have answered these arguments?

2 a) How would you explain the Congress leaders' refusal to be won over by British offers in 1942?
   b) Do you think they were right to refuse?

Unrest

In July 1942 Congress leaders agreed to 'the starting of a mass struggle on non-violent lines on the widest possible scale'.

Protests on a large scale spread across north India in August. Not all were peaceful. Railways, stations, telegraph systems, banks and post offices were wrecked during anti-British riots. But Britain had many troops in the area, gathered to beat off a possible Japanese invasion. These troops put down the 'Quit India' campaign. More than a thousand Indians died, and over 60 000 were arrested, some of whom were punished by being whipped. On at least five occasions crowds were machine-gunned from the air. Congress leaders, including Gandhi and Nehru, were put in prison. While Gandhi was in prison his wife died, and in May 1944 he was released because he was seriously ill.

Some Indian leaders found these years very difficult. Nehru, for example, wished to see the end of the Raj, but did not wish to see Britain's Fascist enemies win victory. Several Congress leaders were personal friends of Labour members of the British Government. But not all Indian nationalists were as cautious as Nehru. Subhas Chandra Bose led those who wanted to use Britain's troubles to win freedom for India. He saw the war as India's opportunity and in 1941 went to Berlin, where he set up a Provisional Government for a free India. In 1943, after Japan had entered the war, he moved to Tokyo. Bose announced to his followers:

> *During the course of this war, Germany, with the help of her allies, has dealt shattering blows to our enemy in Europe – while Japan has inflicted a knockout blow to our enemy in East Asia. Favoured by a most happy combination of circumstances, the Indian people today have a wonderful opportunity for achieving their national emancipation. Having goaded Indians to desperation by its hypocrisy and having driven them to starvation and death by plunder and loot, British rule in India has lost the goodwill of the Indian people. It needs but a flame to destroy the last vestige of that unhappy rule. To light that flame is the task of India's Army of Liberation.*
> Quoted in H. Toye's book, *The Springing Tiger*, 1959

emancipation: freedom

vestige: small amount

Bose built up a force of Indians who called themselves 'The Indian National Army'. According to one of its officers:

> *The INA had only one object and that was to secure the freedom of their country. They did not have very good pay. Nationalist fervour was encouraged by songs about the motherland.*
> Quoted in Z. Masani's book, *Indian Tales of the Raj*, 1987

In fact the INA played little part in the war. In 1945 Bose died in an aircrash and the INA leaders were arrested. However, the British did not execute them as traitors. Many Indians admired their courage and there was some rioting on their behalf in Calcutta.

Questions

1. How might a supporter of Bose have justified the use of force to a follower of Gandhi?

2. Look through Bose's announcement, then describe how he chose his words to influence his followers. Quote examples of words and phrases he used that were aimed to show Britain in a bad light.

In 1945 the Viceroy, Lord Wavell, led yet another unsuccessful attempt to win Indian support. He brought together India's main

Lord Wavell (centre right) visiting an emergency food kitchen in Calcutta during the Bengal famine, 1943. This disaster was mainly the result of the war. Supplies of rice from Burma were cut off and other food supplies were very difficult to move since river boats had been destroyed for fear that the Japanese might advance and capture them. Wavell used troops to tackle the famine, urged the British Government to send food and persuaded Bengal's Governor to introduce rationing.

Right: naval mutineers under arrest in Bombay.

leaders, promised that all his ministers would be Indian, and left them to plan how to decide who would be on his council. They failed. Jinnah claimed that the League alone should choose the Muslim members. Congress refused to agree.

World War II did not end in India in a mood of peace and hope; instead, it ended in a mood of unrest. In February 1946 the Indian Navy mutinied at its base in Bombay, demanding a free India. It put its British officers ashore, steamed out of the harbour and pointed its guns at the city. The British overwhelmed the mutineers, and Congress would not support them. Four days of riots followed in Bombay and naval units at Calcutta, Madras and Karachi mutinied too.

The results of the war

According to Frank Moraes, World War II did benefit India in some ways:

theatre: war zone

> For largely economic reasons a considerable number of Indians were prepared actively to assist the war effort, and there was no shortage of volunteers for the army, which expanded steadily from its peacetime strength. The Indian navy and the Indian air force were also enlarged. India became a supply centre for the mid-eastern theatre. This brought an economic windfall in its wake. Old-established industries producing cotton textiles and jute products were expanded, and with them heavy industries such as steel and cement. The mica industry flourished, and a new wartime venture to manufacture aluminium was built on the country's large bauxite deposits.
>
> These developments affected the minds and emotions of very many Indians, from the villagers transported to the parade ground or factory, to the middle-class urban youths recruited in large numbers, to the expanding bureaucracy and the new emergency officers. Industrial development absorbed many educated Indians in the managerial network of big business or as technicians.
>
> When independence came there were enough Indian officers to take over the armed forces, and a sufficiency of technical and even managerial talent to run the country's commercial and industrial life. Socially, the war brought new habits of discipline, and went some way towards breaking caste prejudices. It also quickened the emancipation of Indian women, a process Gandhi had started when he drew women into active participation in his civil disobedience campaigns.
>
> F. Moraes: *Witness to an Era*, 1973

Question

'The war benefited India.' What evidence of this can you find in the extract from Frank Moraes' book?

The war encouraged Indian nationalism and showed up British weakness: Japan, an Asian power, had been able to defeat British forces. Certainly the League felt that the war had helped them. In 1940 the resignation of Congress members from provincial governments was celebrated as 'a day of deliverance from Congress tyranny'. League members did not resign, and during the war years were able to win control of the provincial governments of Bengal and the North-West Provinces.

In July 1945 British voters went to the polls. They elected a Labour government led by Clement Attlee. The war had done great damage to Britain's finances, trade and economy and the Labour

Party, which had long supported the cause of Indian independence, wished to concentrate on rebuilding British society. Stafford Cripps explained:

After 1945 we were demobilising British Armed Forces as rapidly as was possible, and that meant that the number of British troops which could be left in India and the East was being rapidly diminished.

At the same time, the Indianisation of the Indian Army was proceeding more rapidly than ever. What were the alternatives which faced us? First, we could attempt to strengthen British control in India on the basis of an expanded personnel and a considerable reinforcement of British troops. Such a policy would entail a decision that we should remain in India for at least 15 to 20 years.

The second alternative was, we could make a further attempt to persuade the Indians to come together, while at the same time warning them that there was a limit of time during which we were prepared to maintain our responsibility while awaiting their agreement. One thing that was, I think quite obviously, impossible, was to decide to continue our responsibility indefinitely.

Quoted in C.H. Philips' book, *The Evolution of India and Pakistan*, 1962

New elections were called in India. Congress won 57 of the 102 seats in the Central Assembly. The League won 30 seats. In the provinces Congress had a majority in eight places, the League in three (Sind, Bengal and the Punjab). Britain had lost the desire to stay in charge of India, and in any case was too weak to enforce such a policy. But arranging a peaceful handover of power to an independent India proved as big a problem as any faced by the Raj.

Questions

1 What do you think is the most important reason put forward by Stafford Cripps for British departure from India?

2 What other reasons are mentioned in this chapter?

3 What do you think the British should have done next? Choose one of the following statements, or suggest your own alternative, then give reasons for your answer.
   a) The British should have left at once, without organising India's future.
   b) The British should have stayed and insisted on a united free India.
   c) The British should have stayed to oversee the clash of the League and Congress, trying to keep the peace while the Indians settled their own future.

6 THE END OF BRITISH INDIA

The British Government hoped to bring about a speedy yet peaceful end to the Raj. In fact independence came to India in August 1947 amid dreadful scenes of death and destruction. From the summer of 1946 until well into 1948 violence swept India. At least 200 000 people died as Hindus and Muslims attacked one another in events the British were unable to control.

The worst period of trouble began on 16 August 1946, which the Muslim League declared to be a 'day of direct action' when all Muslims should demonstrate their desire for a separate state for people of their religion. Muslims in Calcutta attacked their Hindu neighbours; Hindus replied with attacks on Muslims. Five thousand people died in events that were witnessed by the British river pilot, Radclyffe Sidebottom:

You could see a crop of one religion or another who had been captured and tied, brought down to the river, being pushed down the bank into the water where dinghies with poles were pushing them under. You could see them being laid on their faces with their heads poking out over Howrah Bridge and being beheaded into the river, their bodies thrown in afterwards. After the riot the river was literally choked with dead bodies which floated for a while, sank for a while and then, when the internal gases blew them up, floated again after three days. They were carried up and down the river by

Police dealing with rioters. Many Indians served as policemen, trying to control fellow Indians who were demonstrating. Why do you think they did this?

the tide, with vultures sitting on their bellies taking bits and leaving the rest to float ashore to be eaten by the dogs, the jackals and the vultures.

Quoted in C. Allen's book, *Plain Tales from the Raj*, 1975

Violence spread through Bengal and Bihar into the North-West Provinces. The horrified British rapidly decided that there was no alternative but to try to divide India, to give Muslims a separate country. Yet in many areas where people of both faiths lived, there was no easy way of dividing the land. In 1947, terrible violence occurred in the Punjab, where sorting out the state's future was especially difficult. The BBC reporter Wynford Vaughan Thomas was there at the time:

I used to see these massacres taking place. People tried to cut people down. It was most extraordinary, in the middle of all these scenes, that nobody for a moment touched me or any European. The trains ran a serious risk. Drivers would shunt into a siding and go off to water the engine. That would give the Sikh bands a chance to come in and they would go right through the train and kill everybody. And the train would then shunt on to Lahore where in a siding they'd have to take the dead out. They were a terrible sight. You could see them coming with the fly swarms around them. And when the bodies were taken out and laid down, there would be about two thousand at a time. One station official turned to me, he'd obviously been used to order — the pride of British India was the railways — and in a voice I will never forget, he said, 'Sire, it is hardly worth issuing tickets anymore.' A good man horrified by the collapse of order.

Quoted in B. Lapping's book, *End of Empire*, 1985

This photograph of a Punjabi town provides evidence of what a riot might do to a community.

Refugees at the fort of Puvaria Quilla, which attracted many Muslims who came to the New Delhi area. What are the refugees carrying? Why did they choose this place?

Swaraj: self-government

Families which felt they were in danger decided to move to areas where people of their own faith were in the majority. Hundreds of thousands of people crammed into trains or trudged slowly along the roads. Rupert Mayne, who had lived in India for many years, watched these refugees as they passed through the Punjab. He recalled:

> *There was mile upon mile of people going East and going West, carrying their belongings. The Hindus and Sikhs moved on one side of the road, the Muslims on the other. We stopped and were watching the people go by when a figure came out of the huge line of refugees, stood to attention, and said he'd been with the 4th Indian Division through the desert and in Italy. What could I do to save him? All I could do was say 'Your politicians asked for 'Swaraj', and this is 'Swaraj'.'*

Quoted in C. Allen's book, *Plain Tales from the Raj*, 1975

Gandhi was appalled by these events. For years he had worked to bring Muslims and Hindus together. Now he travelled to dangerous places in Bihar and East Bengal, and went on a fast in Calcutta in an area where poor Muslims lived. This four-day fast, which started on 1 September 1947, gained much publicity and helped to bring calm to Calcutta. He also visited Delhi. A Hindu shopkeeper remembered how he urged Hindus to accept the new Muslim state of Pakistan that had been created in August 1947 by dividing the area ruled by the British Raj:

He came here after two or three days' trouble and he said: 'If Pakistan is doing wrong and you will do wrong, will two wrongs make one right? Stop all this nonsense. All the Mohammedans are Indians, your brothers, and they have lived here for all these years, so they must not be put in trouble and no firing and no killing, nothing should be done.' It was stopped. All this was stopped after about two days' preaching.

Quoted in F.W. Watson and H. Tennyson's book, *Talking of Gandhi*, 1969

As refugees finally settled in the two new countries of India and Pakistan, so the violence at last began to fade away.

Questions

1 From your studies so far, why do you think the worst violence occurred in the areas mentioned above?

2 Using the sources in the above section, write a letter from a refugee to his or her relatives. In your letter mention your reasons for leaving, the place you hope to go to, and the adventures you have experienced on the way.

3 a) What arguments did Gandhi use against violence?
   b) What does his success in Calcutta reveal about most Indians' feelings towards him?

Independence – the plan

Lord and Lady Mountbatten with Gandhi at the Viceroy's House, Delhi, in March 1947. Gandhi did not play a central role in the planning of India's future in 1946–7. He disliked the idea of partition and was deeply distressed by the violence that developed.

The British had originally hoped to leave India in June 1948. In March 1947 Lord Wavell was replaced as Viceroy by Lord Louis Mountbatten, a relative of the British royal family and an important military leader who had risen to be Supreme Allied Commander of South-East Asia during World War II. Mountbatten was confident, charming and a very skilled negotiator. He soon established friendly relations with Nehru. He had, moreover, enormous power to negotiate as he thought best.

The violence that Mountbatten could see around him made him decide that Britain must pull out in 1947, not 1948, and that the Muslims must be given a separate state – 'Pakistan'. One of Mountbatten's officials explained:

In his first talks with Lord Mountbatten the Muslim League leader, Mr Jinnah, gave a frank warning that unless an acceptable political solution was reached very quickly he could not guarantee to control the situation from his side. A similar warning was given by Congress leaders.

Unity had been Britain's greatest achievement in India, but by March 1947 the only alternatives were Pakistan or chaos. Lord Mountbatten discovered from personal discussions with the leaders of the Muslim League that they would insist on partition at all costs and fight a civil war rather than accept transfer of power to a Hindu majority union, while Congress showed themselves as champions of unity, but not at the price of coercion.

coercion: force

Quoted in A. Campbell-Johnson's book, *Mission with Mountbatten*, 1951

Through discussions with leading Indians, and the work of his own staff (especially an Indian called V.P. Menon), a plan for the future emerged.

Once the Indian leaders had accepted the plan, Mountbatten persuaded them to broadcast their acceptance on the radio. However, all these negotiations did not include the princely states, and Mountbatten now tried to persuade these states to merge with either India or Pakistan. An ICS officer in one of the states wrote of Mountbatten:

He applied the whole force of his immense prestige and his unique powers of persuasion to securing the assent of the rulers to new agreements that would permanently subordinate them to the successor Governments of India and Pakistan. Except in the case of two or

subordinate: place them under the control of

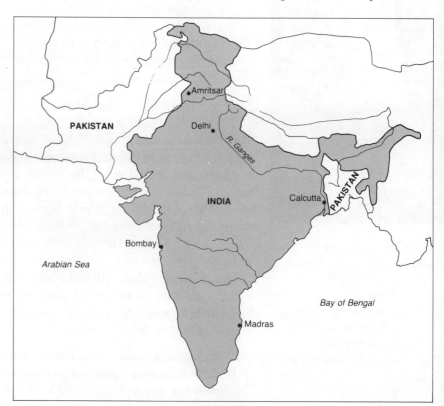

The new states of India and Pakistan, 1947. How does this map compare with the one on page 39 that shows the areas where most Muslims lived?

three States, the pressure that he exercised proved effective. The Princes of India signed their own death warrants and their States disappeared from the face of the map. Once allies of the Crown, they are now pensioners of a Republic.

Quoted in E. Wakefield's book, *Past Imperative*, 1966

In Hyderabad and Junagadh the Muslim rulers of largely Hindu states only joined India after Indian troops had moved into their lands. In the far north Kashmir, ruled by a Hindu but with a population that was over 70 per cent Muslim, had frontiers with both countries. It was to prove a source of conflict in years to come. The princes allowed the governments of India and Pakistan to control defence, foreign affairs and communications, just as the British Raj had done, but they were not confident of keeping their other powers. In India especially they were proved correct. Soon the maharajahs were virtually without power. In Dhrangadhara the Maharajah recalled what happened when he told his people that their state was now part of the new India:

There was stunned silence when I told them that what we had done was for their interest, and that it would be a more economic kind of government and a more co-operative situation would prevail. Nobody had any comment to make and only one person, an elderly village head, said to me, 'That is all very well Sir, I know what you have done, but who will now wipe our tears?' I was so taken aback by that one and only remark that I was not able to proceed any further with the meeting and I left, but I did feel that it had been a tribute not necessarily to me alone, but to my whole line — that they had wiped tears in their time.

Quoted in C. Allen's book, *The Lives of the Indian Princes*, 1984

Questions

1 Why did Mountbatten believe in a speedy end to the Raj and in a divided India?

2 If you had been opposed to a divided India, what might you have said against the plan that was agreed? (Search for all the weaknesses and try to work out what the future problems might be.)

3 Do you think that the ICS officer who wrote the account of Mountbatten and the princes approved of the Viceroy's actions? Give reasons for your answer.

4 a) What does the Maharajah's report on his people's behaviour reveal about their feelings towards him?
   b) Can you think of any reason to doubt the truth of what the Maharajah said?

Independence – the right approach?

For a brief moment on 15 August 1947 India forgot its troubles and celebrated the end of the Raj. An Indian journalist wrote:

I happened to be outside the Parliament House when Nehru made his speech. It was an enormous crowd and somehow one had forgotten all about what we'd been through and the killing and the riots. One felt very elated: at long last the country was free and we could manage our own affairs. Next morning...the Mountbattens went in their horse-drawn carriage to the Red Fort; I couldn't believe it, the crowd took the horses away and dragged his carriage themselves, cheering the British. Staid, stiff British officers in uniforms were lifted shoulder high and cheered. It seemed that a hundred and fifty years of bitterness, the massacre at Amritsar, all the civil disobedience movements and all the anti-British feelings had totally vanished and this nation had become more pro-British than it had ever been since the British came.

Quoted in B. Lapping's book, *End of Empire*, 1985

elated: very happy

Jawaharlal Nehru, India's first Prime Minister, in London in 1946. Compare his style of dress with that adopted by Gandhi on his visit to London in 1931. Why do they differ so much?

Both India and Pakistan agreed to join the Commonwealth, but the two countries did not become friends; Kashmir, especially, remained a cause of conflict between them. Jinnah and the League were delighted with partition. They believed that they had saved the Muslims from being ruled over by Hindus. But some Muslims disagreed with them. The leader of the Kashmir Muslims, Sheikh Muhammad Abdullah, feared that Pakistan would split apart. He said:

In spite of ideas of Muslims being one community, differences between the different units of Pakistan are bound to come to the forefront.

Quoted in B.N. Pandey's book, *The Indian Nationalist Movement*, 1974

Pakistan's first Prime Minister, Leaquat Ali Khan, signing an oath of loyalty to Pakistan. Jinnah, the Governor General of the new country, watches. By now Jinnah was seriously ill. He died in September 1948.

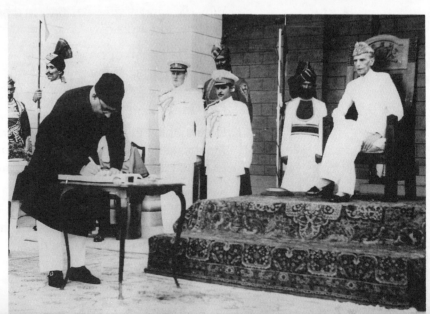

The Indian armed forces of the Raj, and the ICS, had to be split between the two new countries. There were Indians who thought that the British stood aside from all the divisions, confusions and violence of this time, when they could have done more. One of these Indians, Khushwant Singh, thought that the British attitude was very much along the lines of:

'You stew in your own juice. You didn't want us: now you look after yourselves.' There was a certain amount of malicious pleasure in seeing that we were at each other's throats. They said 'We told you that you can't run your own country; see what's happening.' So they kept aloof.
   Quoted in Z. Masani's book, *Indian Tales of the Raj*, 1987

But Mountbatten believed that the British were powerless to prevent the violence of 1946−8. In a report written in September 1948, he argued:

It is doubtful whether more could have been done had more time been available. British troops were not used. The instructions of Government were that they were only to be used to protect European lives. No Indian leader would have agreed [to use British troops]. Military action alone cannot stop large-scale disturbances in the Indian sub-continent. The form of the disturbances and the areas involved make the soldiers' task an almost impossible one.
   Quoted in H.V. Hodson's book, *The Great Divide*, 1969

On 30 January 1948 the violence claimed the life of Gandhi himself. His death was witnessed by Robert Stimpson, a BBC correspondent. He reported:

Mr Gandhi came out of Birla House and because he was a little late for evening prayers, he stepped more briskly than at any time since his fast. He was wearing his usual white loin-cloth and a pair of sandals. He had thrown a shawl round his chest for it was getting chilly. His arms were resting lightly on the shoulders of two companions and he was smiling. There were only two or three hundred people in the garden and they pressed eagerly towards him as he climbed the steps leading to the lawn where the congregation had gathered. As he got to the top of the steps and approached the crowd he took his arms from the shoulders of his friends and raised his hands in salutation. He was still smiling. A thick-set man, in his thirties I should say and dressed in khaki, was in the forefront of the crowd. He moved a step towards Mr Gandhi, took out a revolver and fired several shots.
   Quoted in F.W. Watson and H. Tennyson's book, *Talking of Gandhi*, 1969

Gandhi's killer was a man called N.V. Godse. He belonged to the fanatical group Hindu Mahasabha, who feared that Gandhi was destroying the purity of their faith.

Gandhi's funeral. Nehru told the Indian people that Gandhi's death meant 'the light has gone from our lives'.

Questions

1. a) Find and list any arguments which suggest that the British did not handle the ending of the Raj as well as they might have done.
   b) What arguments did Mountbatten offer in his own defence?
   c) Which do you find the more convincing?

2. How might an Indian or Pakistani newspaper have reported the coming of independence? Under a suitable headline, write a report mentioning the feelings of the people, your own views on the events, and what you think the future holds for your country.

The British rule that Gandhi had helped to end had been an astonishing achievement, given the size of India. It was made possible, in part, by divisions between Indians; those divisions had led to the emergence of two independent countries, not the united land that Gandhi had wished to see. Both of these countries were to face vast challenges in the future.

Coursework assignment: from the Raj to independence

The following assignment is intended to focus attention on a number of key events and to develop particular skills required in examinations.

a) **Skill: selection, arrangement and presentation of relevant knowledge**
   (i) List the main events that explain why the Raj was ready to share so much of its power in the 1935 India Act.
   (ii) Choose the event which seems to you to be the most important and give a brief account of it, explaining its importance (in about 200 words).

b) **Skill: understanding historical terminology and concepts**
   (i) Give a brief definition of two of the following terms:
      a) Imperialism; b) Dyarchy; c) Partition;
      d) Repression; e) Civil disobedience.
   (ii) Draw upon evidence from the period to illustrate your definitions, then explain their importance.

c) **Skill: evaluation of source material**

   A Frank Moraes' reflections on the results of British rule:

   British-trained Indian officers of the army, navy and air force were able to carry on the military training and traditions inherited from foreign rulers.

   The development of transport might have been undertaken to serve British interests, but they also helped to bring the villages of rural India into closer touch with the towns and cities. This assisted industrialization. ... trade got a considerable fillip from the two world wars — although the incentive was the urgency to meet Britain's military needs, in the long run India benefited.

   The urge for political freedom was a reaction to British rule, and the idea of political liberty spread to India largely from the liberal writings and speeches of British historians, scholars, politicians and thinkers. Until the British came, democracy was largely unknown in India. So were nationalism and industrialization, modern science and technology.

   But one thing they failed to do: they failed to open a line of genuine communication on a basis of personal equality between themselves and the new Indian middle class they had created. The British treated the educated classes with suspicion, preferring to deal with the ignorant, indigent Indian.

   F. Moraes: *Witness to an Era*, 1973

fillip: boost

indigent: poor

B Nehru's reflections:

consolidate: secure

[The British] opposed all who worked for political and social change. The introduction of the railway was intended to consolidate their rule for their own benefit. British rule created classes and interests which were tied up with that rule. There were the landowners and the princes and members of departments of government. Government was run on an extravagant scale, all the highly paid positions being reserved for Europeans. To this must be added the policy of creating divisions among Indians, of encouraging one group at the cost of another. Nearly all our major problems have grown up during British rule: the princes, the lack of industry and the neglect of agriculture, the tragic poverty of the people.

J. Nehru: *The Discovery of India*, 1946

(i) Notice the date of source **B**. What were the circumstances in India when Nehru expressed these opinions?

(ii) Are there any issues on which the authors of these sources seem to be in agreement?

(iii) What are the main differences in the views expressed in these two sources?

(iv) Do you think that one of these sources is more valuable than the other? Discuss the value of the sources (in the light of who wrote them) to explain your answer.

d) **Skill: analysis of continuity and change**

(i) How do you account for the Congress leaders' acceptance of the partition of India in 1947, in view of the party's earlier views?

(ii) Gandhi believed in peaceful protest throughout this period. Do you think his methods were more appropriate at some times rather than others? Or, was he either always right or always unrealistic? Give reasons for your answer.

e) **Skill: empathy**

Imagine you are a journalist interviewing an elderly Indian prince whose state has just been merged into independent India or Pakistan.

(i) What sort of questions would you wish to ask the maharajah?

(ii) Suggest the kind of answers the maharajah might have given to your questions.

Skills grid

Key
- **U** Using the evidence
- **Q** Questions
- **C** Coursework assignment

A Historical skills

1 Using historical evidence

	U 7	U 10	U 16	Q 21	Q 23	Q 27	Q 28	Q 31	Q 36	Q 39	U 44	Q 48	U 49	U 59	C 61
Comprehension of variety of sources	■		■		■	■			■	■	■			■	■
Extraction of information				■					■	■			■	■	■
Evaluation, recognising * fact *v* opinion					■									■	■
* bias		■	■												
* importance of origin and context		■													
Recognition of inference and implication in a source	■						■	■	■					■	■
Comparison of different sources based on relative reliability								■	■				■	■	■
Reaching conclusions on basis of this comparison								■							■
Recognizing gaps and inconsistencies				■											
Judgement and choice between various opinions															
Formation of overview and synthesis of one's own opinion											■	■			

2 Empathy

Understanding events and issues from perspective of people in the past												■	■		

B Historical concepts

Cause and consequence	■													■	■
Continuity and change	■						■	■							■
Similarity and difference					■										
Time, sequence and chronology									■					■	■
Interaction of individual with society				■											
Historical vocabulary and terminology			■												■

INDEX

Numerals in **bold** denote illustrations

Ahmad Khan, Sir Sayid, 40, 41
Aligarh College, 41, 42
Ambedkar, B.R., 32
Amritsar, 17–25, **17**, 28, **31**, 33, 58
army, 8, 13, **13**, 14, 17, 18, 19, 20, **46**
Arya Samaj, 40
Attlee, C., 50

Besant, Annie, 26, 27
Bose, Subhas Chandra, 33, 48

Calcutta, **15**, 16, 34, 38, 48, 49, 52, 54
Chauri Chaura, **31**, 32
Churchill, Winston, 34
Congress Party, 24, 26–37, 40, 41, 42, 43, 44, 46, 51, 56
Cripps, Sir Stafford, **44**, 47, 51
Curzon, Lord, 6, 7, 9, 10, 12

disease, 11, 19, 27
Dufferin, Lord, 26, 27
dyarchy, 25, 37, 61
Dyer, General, **17**, 19, **19**, 20, 21, **22**, 23, **23**, 24

education, 9, 10, 12, 13, 26, 61

Gandhi, M.K., 27–35, **28**, 40, 42, 44, 47, 50, 54–5, **55**, 59, 60, **60**, 62
Godse, N.V., 59
Gokhale, G.K., 27
Golden Temple, 18

hartal, 30
Hinduism, 12, 32, 38–9, 40, 42, 52
Hindu Mahasabha, 40, 59

Hunter Commission, 20, 22, 25
Hyderabad, **5**, 57

India Act 1909, 27, 41
India Act 1919, 25
India Act 1935, 36, 37, 46
Indian Civil Service, 8, 9, **9**, 10, 26, 56, 57, 59
Indian National Army, 48
industries, 10, 11, 13, 33, 50, 61
Irwin, Lord, 32, 34

Jallianwala Bagh, 18, **18**, 19, 20, 24
Japan, 47, 48, 49, 50
Jinnah, M.A., 42–5, **43**, **44**, 55, **58**

Kashmir, 57, 58
khaddar, 29, 32
Khilafat, 42
Koran, 39

Lahore Resolution, 44–5
Lee Commission, 9
Linlithgow, Lord, 46, 47
Lucknow Pact, 43

maharajahs, 5, **6**, 7, 13, 57, 62
Minto, Lord, 27, **41**, 41
Moguls, 39
Montagu, Edwin, 22, **23**, 24, 27
Moplahs, 38, 42
Morley, John, 27, 41
Mountbatten, Lord Louis, 55–60, **55**, **60**
Muslims, 12, 19, 32, 35, 38–9, **39**, 40, 41, 42, 43, 52, 53, 54, 55, 57, 58
Muslim League, 37, 41–5, 50, 52, 56, 58

naval mutiny, 49, **49**

Nehru, J., 24, 28, 33, 34, 36, 44, 47, 48, 55, **58**, **58**, 62

O'Dwyer, Sir Michael, 19, 21, 24, 25

Pakistan, 54, 55, 56, **56**, 58, **58**
Peshawar, **15**, 33
Princely States, **5**, 6, 7, 25, 37, 56–7, 62
Punjab, 18, 19, 20, 23, 24, 39, 51, 53, **53**, 54
punkah wallah, **14**

'Quit India' campaign, 47

railways, 9, 11, 13, 26, 47, 53, 62
rioting, 38, 46, 47, 49, 52–3, **52**
Round Table Conference, 35
Rowlatt laws, 19, 20, 26, 28
ryots, 30

salt tax, 30
Sèvres, Treaty of, 41
Sherwood, Marcia, 19, 22, **22**
Sikhs, 12, 18, 24, 39, 40, 53, 54
Simon Commission, 34
Suez Canal, 14
Swaraj, 26, 54

Tilak, B.G., 27
Turkey, 41

untouchables, **12**, 31, 35, 40

Viceroys, 6, **8**, 9, 25, 26, 27, 32, 34, 37, 41, 43, 44, 48, 55

Wavell, Lord, 48, **49**, 55
World War I, 13, 28, 41
World War II, 46, 50, 55